Niche Marketing FOR COACHES

Hannah McNamara

Viva Books

New Delhi | Mumbai | Chennai | Kolkata | Bangalore | Hyderabad | Kochi

First Indian Edition 2008

VIVA BOOKS PRIVATE LIMITED

- 4737/23 Ansari Road, Daryaganj, New Delhi 110 002
  E-mail: vivadelhi@vivagroupindia.net, Tel. 42242200
- Plot No. 76, Service Industries, Shirvane, Sector 1, Nerul, Navi Mumbai 400 706
  E-mail: vivamumbai@vivagroupindia.net, Tel. 27721273, 27721274
- Jamals Fazal Chambers, 26 Greams Road, Chennai 600 006
  E-mail: vivachennai@vivagroupindia.net, Tel. 28290304, 28294241
- B-103, Jindal Towers, 21/1A/3 Darga Road, Kolkata 700 017
  E-mail: vivakolkata@vivagroupindia.net, Tel. 22836381, 22816713
- 7, Sovereign Park Apartments, 56-58, K. R. Road, Basavanagudi, Bangalore 560 004
  E-mail: vivabangalore@vivagroupindia.net, Tel. 26607409, 26607410
- 101-102 Mughal Marc Apartments, 3-4-637 to 641, Narayanguda, Hyderabad 500 029
  E-mail: vivahyderabad@vivagroupindia.net, Tel. 27564481, 27564482
- Beevi Towers, First Floor, SRM Road, Kaloor, Kochi 682 018, Kerala
  E-mail: vivakochi@vivagroupindia.net, Tel: 0484-2403055, 2403056

www.vivagroupindia.com

Published by arrangement with

Thorogood Publishing
10-12, Rivington Street,
London EC2A 3DU

ISBN-10: 81-309-0847-6
ISBN-13: 978-81-309-0847-2

Published by Vinod Vasishtha for Viva Books Private Limited, 4737/23, Ansari Road, New Delhi-110 002. Printed and bound by Anand Sons, Delhi - 110 092.

Praise for Niche Marketing For Coaches and Hannah McNamara

"Essential reading for anyone who's serious about running a life coaching, executive coaching or business coaching practice."

Jonathan Jay, founder of The Coaching Academy and author of 'Sack Your Boss'.

"Hannah McNamara is a successful coach who has the rare quality of actually walking her talk. In her informative new book she shares secrets of success drawn from coaching and marketing. Hannah provides valuable tools in an easy to read, step-by-step format that is also straightforward to apply. A must read for all Coaches."

Caroline Shola Arewa, Health and Success Coach, speaker and author of 'Embracing Purpose, Passion and Peace'.

"This book needs to be in the hands of every coach. Hannah is a master marketeer and knows exactly what coaches need to grasp about the business they love. Be prepared to discover insider secrets for attracting clients and discovering your specialist niche area. This book will not only give you the practical tools to generate the success you deserve, but also motivates you to make this happen sooner, rather than later. Hannah's wise tips and advice compelled me to take full advantage of the marketing opportunities available to me as soon as I finished the first few chapters. The results were astonishing. A must read for all coaches who refuse to settle for mediocrity and are going for gold – an outstanding coaching business, suited to their own unique personality and expertise. At last a coaching book about marketing know-how!"

Shilpa Unalkat, author of 'Corporate Head, Spiritual Heart' www.staflow.com

"As a coach Hannah exceeded all of my expectations: I felt supported throughout the process; I was never made to feel out of my depth; I was encouraged but also challenged; I learnt a great deal about marketing and being a great coach. Each session was structured and calm but also dynamic and motivating. It gave me a clear focus for

understanding marketing whilst also helping me to develop my business ideas. Every single coaching session was about results and therefore in only three months I have made the significant leap from having a vague business idea to actually running a business!"

Charlotte Hunter, Coach.

"Hannah is a pleasure to work with. She instantly tunes into the issues which are relevant at that particular time. Her advice is sound and practical which inspires confidence. I had seen Hannah speak live and remember well how she impressed me with her knowledge of marketing through magazines and newspapers. I'd recommend her to anyone wishing to learn from someone who really knows what they are talking about."

Susan Goss, Coach.

"I was feeling desperate and frustrated. If you do not market your business, you do not have a business. The sessions were very organized and I made steady progress through to the amazing array of possibilities available."

Patricia Stuart-Tuck, Coach (www.pst-LifeCoaching.co.uk).

"Hannah, thanks so much for the session today on PR. I came to it hoping for some tips on how best to approach PR for my coaching practice and came away with a complete breakthrough! I have just reeled off a list of specific markets and publications I intend to target, I have tons of ideas to explore and a thirst for more networking. Most importantly, I've reached the realization that a lot of this is common sense and I have all the tools I need to achieve regular press coverage in all the right places. Thanks again for letting me pick your considerably knowledgeable brain!"

Lisa Ravenscroft, Coach.

"Thanks very much for the coaching you have given me on marketing my business. As you are aware I had a quiet spell in April this year but since discussing the challenge with you, receiving some excellent tips, being motivated and more disciplined, I am now in a much stronger position. I would recommend you to anyone in a similar position."

John Benedict, Coach.

"Prior to engaging Hannah, I already believed in the power of coaching as an agent of positive change. However, my coaching sessions with Hannah have reinforced my original viewpoint. Hannah asks the right questions at the right time. Moreover, she skillfully reframed specific challenges that I was facing. This made it much easier for me to identify ways in which I could overcome these challenges. I would wholeheartedly recommend that if you're considering employing a coach, you start by contacting Hannah."

Alex Reid, Coach.

To Pat, my ever supportive husband

Acknowledgements

Many people have contributed to my being able to write this book – some directly and some indirectly, and it is impossible to thank them all. Along the way there have been mentors, professional advisors and true friends who have steered me in the right direction and inspired me to go for it.

To the many coaches who I have had the pleasure to train with, work with and to share marketing successes (and 'learning experiences') with, I couldn't have done it without you.

My particular thanks go to Yvette Bennett, Jenny Chalmers, Angela Dunbar and Joanne Murphy who have assisted me in the preparation of this book and the niche coaches – Guy Levine, Chris Barrows, Nicola Cairncross, Joanne Mallon and Judith Morgan – who have contributed with interviews.

Hannah McNamara

Contents

FOUR

SECTION 2 START SHOOTING THOSE DUCKS!

FIVE

NINE

Introduction

Introduction

Coaching is said to be one of the fastest growing professions.

Lifestyle magazines run articles about coaching and personal development and there are life coaches on the radio and on TV. Celebrities are publicly thanking their coaches for their support, business people are acknowledging their coaches when they have achieved success and conference speakers talk about coaching as being one of the most useful management tools.

There are Life Coaches, Work/Life Balance Coaches, Relationship Coaches, Career Coaches, Parent Coaches, Executive Coaches, Small Business Coaches, Presentation Skills Coaches, Leadership Coaches… the list goes on.

Everyone seems to be talking about coaching and many people, like you, want to be a successful professional coach.

The biggest taboo in coaching…

Whilst coaches are in training, they experience coaching for themselves and they discover that it can have a profound impact on people's quality of life, probably more so than they would have imagined before they started their studies.

Friends are made on the course, people keep in touch and it feels good to be around others who can talk in an educated way about coaching models, techniques and experiences with clients.

As coaches become more involved in the coaching community, they hear success stories and 'rags to riches' tales of coaches who have 'made it big'. People are talking about hourly rates of £50, £100 and sometimes even £500! It's exciting to think that anything is possible and coaching offers not only the chance to work in a very rewarding profession, but to achieve financial security.

Everything is building to that magical day when the certificate or diploma arrives. The day that you can say with confidence, *"I'm a qualified coach."*

Around this time, many new coaches decide to launch their new coaching practice. The desk is set up, the phone line is installed and the business cards are in their shiny new business card holder ready to give out to anyone who asks, *"I'm thinking about working with a coach, do you know anyone?"*

But next comes the part that we don't talk about – it's the biggest taboo in coaching. The phone doesn't ring all by itself. People walking past your home don't telepathically know that there's a coach inside who could help them to achieve their goals. For new coaches who have not been in business for themselves before, and even seasoned professionals, it can be daunting to think about ways to start spreading the word about your new coaching practice and start attracting clients.

Marketing coaching is different

Even if, like me, you've spent all of your career working in marketing (see later), it can be a shock to discover that marketing coaching is not like marketing a can of baked beans or any other packaged good or product. Coaching is intangible – people can't see, hear or touch what it's going to be like when they buy. They can only experience it. Clients are taking a big risk when they decide to work with a coach because they have to take your word for what they'll get from it. For this reason, trust is a much larger factor in a client's decision to work with a particular coach than it is for many other purchasing decisions.

Some very successful marketing professionals who have made the transition to being independent coaches have found that the techniques and strategies that worked for them before don't work now. Why? Well, very often they have been successful at marketing an established product or service. Something that is known to its buyers and has an element of goodwill attached to it. When you're starting a service-based business from scratch it takes time to build up a brand and goodwill.

Hannah's background

I was lucky when I came to starting up as a coach because I already had a background in marketing and business. I also had experience of selling to companies. That's one of the reasons I decided to write this book – the majority of people starting off as coaches have come from very different backgrounds and don't enjoy marketing as much as I do.

My story is that I started off in retail sales and then after completing a four-year university degree in Business Studies (I specialized in marketing), I worked for a sales promotion agency, a PR agency and a generalist marketing consultancy before moving 'client-side' to the marketing department of a well-known womenswear and home furnishings retailer.

Over the next four years, I looked after the full spectrum of marketing activities from direct marketing, advertising, PR and in-store promotions to organizing exhibition stands and new store openings. I then moved into the male-dominated cut-throat world of electrical retail where I ran the marketing department. There I held together and developed a team of eager marketing professionals whilst we had the threat of redundancy hanging over our heads. When the redundancies did happen, I moved into magazine publishing and helped to launch a new glossy magazine, then took a gap year with my husband and worked in publishing in Australia. (I also did lots of other short-term jobs like door-to-door sales, a driving job, worked in a clothes shop and even was the 'face' of a recruitment consultancy when I posed as a midwife in their press adverts!)

When I met some coaches while I was away, I realized that I had been using coaching techniques as a manager for some time, before they had been labelled as such, and when I returned to the UK, I decided to study for a coaching qualification with The Coaching Academy.

I then set up a coaching practice where I worked with a group of experienced coaches and I concentrated on Business Development – going out and getting the clients. Within three months we had our first corporate client which was an international PR firm. The practice has grown from there and now most of our clients are people working in professional services firms.

Along the way there have been good times and tough times, and I've learned a lot about what works and what doesn't when promoting a coaching practice.

In addition to running my practice, I launched a specialist website for coaches who want to learn more about marketing: www.marketinghelpforcoaches.com – and I am one of the marketing trainers at The Coaching Academy. I work on a one-to-one basis with new coaches to help them launch their coaching practices. I think that good marketing is absolutely essential for new coaches and in this book you'll discover some of the secrets about getting your message out there.

About this book

This book is about getting started as a professional coach. But it goes beyond just talking about getting started because in this book you'll find the tools you need to identify your target clients, establish your own personal brand and develop a marketing strategy.

Comfort zones

Would I be right in thinking that at least once, you've needed to challenge a client to step out of their comfort zone to do something that's going to help them to achieve their goal? You might say to that client that unless they're prepared to take action and do something, nothing will change – *"if you always do what you've always done, you'll always get what you've always got."*

It's the same with this book.

Practically everything you need to start getting coaching clients is in here. But it's your responsibility to do something about it – I can't make you. It's one thing to know what you should do, it's quite another to actually do it.

If you're serious about being a professional coach, then from time to time, perhaps every single day, you'll need to stretch or even smash your comfort zones.

And if that makes you uncomfortable...it should. That's the idea!

Wealth warning

The chances are that if you're thinking about becoming, or you already are, a professional full-time coach, then you'll either have already given up the day job or it's on the horizon.

The stark reality is that, unless you are already 'financially free', if you are giving up a regular pay-check, you are going to need to achieve a certain level of income from coaching. In a nutshell, you need to make a *living* as a coach.

Whatever your beliefs about money, in this material world you do need money to live. Money has been around as a means of trade for thousands of years and it's not going away.

Despite our best efforts, positive intent and 'giving something back' does not pay the mortgage or the gas bill. And whilst you might be able to barter coaching for other products or services, you can't use it to buy petrol, food or your favourite treats.

This book is about finding ways to get clients who **pay you** to coach them. If this offends you, then please stop reading right now because you're going to be even more offended as you read on!

Get rich quick

Very, very few people are an overnight success as a coach. This book will **not** help you to get rich quick. In fact, if you want to be a professional coach, prepare yourself for the long-haul. Unless you have a book of contacts that are ready to start using your services, expect to have to support yourself for your first year.

That's right, it can take up to a year (sometimes more) of hard work to earn a good, regular income from coaching. I don't say that to scare you, but I say it because I think you chose this book and you want me to be honest with you. However, if you're prepared to stretch your comfort zones and be bold, you can definitely accelerate the process. This book will show you what you need to do, step by step.

Assumptions

When I sat down to write this book, I had to make a few assumptions that may or may not be true about you:

- You're studying for or have already completed a good, solid coach training programme and are familiar with basic NLP (Neuro-Linguistic Programming) techniques
- You have some practical experience of coaching people
- You'd like to have more paying coaching clients
- You have little or no prior experience of marketing a professional practice
- You're prepared to try new things
- You have someone you trust who can coach you to overcome any fears, limiting beliefs or blocks that might be holding you back
- You have access to someone who can advise you on the legalities and tax implications of starting your own business
- You want me to be straight with you

Finding your way around

This book is organized into sections that go into greater depth about each aspect of marketing yourself as a coach. This means that you can dip in and out as you need to and gloss over any ideas that you might already be using in your coaching practice. You may find it helpful to keep a pad and pen with you so you can work through the exercises straight away.

Section 1 Getting Your Ducks in a Row

Before you start spending money on marketing, there is some ground work to be done – ground work that will help you to set your goals for your coaching practice and the marketing you do to support it.

In this section, you'll discover:

- How to use coaching tools for marketing
- What Marketing actually is (and it's not selling or advertising)
- How to choose a niche that suits you
- The importance of experience, credibility and contacts
- The three phases of launching a coaching practice
- How good branding can make a big impact
- What the 'going rate' is for coaches
- How much you should charge

Once you've worked through this section, you'll be clear about the kinds of people who you want to attract with your marketing and those marketing efforts will generate much better results.

chapter one Using Coaching Tools

ONE Using Coaching Tools

You already know the answer

As a coach, you know that the client is a resourceful individual and that they already have the answers inside of them. Your job as a coach is to help them to bring those answers to the surface.

You already know how best to market yourself as a coach, but you may not realize it.

In this chapter, I'd like to reintroduce you to some of the coaching tools you're already familiar with, but we'll be using them in a marketing context.

We'll use a variation of the Wheel of Life, the GROW model and elements of NLP.

As you become used to using these tools for marketing, you'll develop a good understanding about what's special about *you* as a coach, and how you can help your clients – so you get that message across to people in a really powerful and compelling way and you'll start to attract clients.

Now, whether that's pro-bono practice clients to start off with, whether it's paying clients ... whether it's attracting the *right* kind of paying clients – this book is going to give you the tools that *you need* to go out there and attract some people, and get your coaching practice off the ground.

Do you have a pad and pen handy? I'd suggest that you keep a pad and pen with you as you go through this book because there are some exercises and you'll probably want to jot down your thoughts as you go.

I'm going to be sharing with you some of the methods that I've used to launch my own coaching practice, the things that *actually work*.

Before we talk about the Coaching Tools, let's take a moment to think about what marketing really is.

What is marketing?

If you open any text book, you'll come across some very fancy definitions of marketing. And, it's always something along the lines of 'Meeting customers' needs *profitably*'.

If you ask the general population, they will probably include one or more of the following in their answer:

- Advertising
- Public Relations (PR)
- Direct mail or sales letters
- Websites

And these are all *parts* of marketing, but they're *not* the whole story.

When you look into 'What marketing is' the classical school of thought on marketing is that there are four 'P's'.

- Product
- Price
- Place and
- Promotion

What most people think of, when they talk of marketing, is the promotion aspect of it. The other P's are hidden. They are happening behind the scenes, but that doesn't mean that they're any less important. In fact, I'd argue that there's no point even starting on promotion until you're clear about the other P's.

More recently, marketing professionals have added a further three P's to the marketing mix:

- People
- Process
- Physical evidence

Let's go through each of the P's one by one.

Product

Coaching is not a physical product. Because it's an interaction between two people, you can't manufacture it in advance and show it to someone. They can't examine it in detail before they decide to buy. But that doesn't mean that you can't present it in a way that people understand. The more that you can be clear about what you're offering to your clients and how it's different, the easier it is for clients to 'get it'. So:

- What exactly is it that you're offering to your client?
- What's special about *you*?
- How can you package up your services?
- Do you only want to be offering one-to-one coaching? Or, do you want to do *group work*?
- Do you want to run workshops? Open seminars?
- Do you want to coach people by *e-mail*?
- Could you use *e-books*?
- Could you use *audio products*?
- Do you offer your clients any money-back guarantees?

There are all sorts of different options available for you, and even once you've got your product right, that's not the whole story because you need to price it.

Price

Pricing isn't just a matter of plucking a figure out of the air. The *more* that you understand your marketplace, the *easier* it is going to be when you're starting to set your prices. And this is pricing for:

- One-off sessions
- Packages
- Different options on telephone coaching
- Face-to-face coaching

Price says a lot about the way you position yourself in the marketplace, and also the kind of clients that you want to attract. Further information is provided on pricing in Chapter 4.

Place

The place is much more than the actual premises you use to coach from. It includes:

- The places that you'll be seen
- The company you keep
- The places that people would search for information about coaching.

Promotion

This is how you communicate your offering to the outside world. Where a company offering a product would rely on advertising and sales letters, promotion for a service such as coaching is done in a different way. But more about that later!

People

This means the people that your client interacts with as you market yourself and deliver your service. If you use a virtual assistant or call answering service to take incoming calls, they are acting on *your* behalf. Are they doing a good job of representing your coaching practice? As you grow, you may take on a receptionist or someone to do your business development. Again, are they representing you well?

Process

This is about how you operate your coaching practice and includes:

- How exactly do you deliver your service?
- What's the process for a new client?
- Do you have a standard set of forms that they need to fill in?

Physical evidence

As I said in the introduction, it's risky for clients when they first take you on because they don't know what to expect. What can you do to demonstrate to them that you are a professional and you're able to do a good job? Consider:

- Testimonials
- Case studies
- Coaching environment: Does it appear professional?
- Are your qualifications and public liability insurance certificates on display?
- Marketing materials: do they portray the right image?

The secret to effective service marketing

All of the Seven P's are important. But there's something else that goes to the very heart of what effectively marketing services is about; it's something that you already know about.

And that's *rapport*.

Marketing is a way of building rapport with our clients, before we've even met them or spoken to them. It's a way of connecting with our clients on a deep level – so that when they see your marketing message, when they hear about you, when they attend a workshop, they do feel that connection with you. So that there is no other choice than choosing you as their coach, because you already have that powerful chemistry with them.

But the only way that you can create that rapport is if you truly understand your target market. Who are the people that you really, really want to attract through your marketing?

Now, the great thing is that you learn how to build rapport with people as part of your coach training. You're taught all sorts of different tools – whether it's through body language, through tonality or through using the right sort of language with people. These can also translate into your marketing, and I'm going to show you '*how*' a bit later on.

Before we do that, it's time for your first exercise.

The wheel of marketing

You can either use the wheel that is on the following page or you can use your pad and pen – I'll leave that up to you. On the wheel, mark where you think your level of knowledge is, right now, for each of the subjects listed on a scale of 0 to 10 where:

10 means that you know everything there is to know thank you very much, and you're supremely confident that you're already applying everything.

5 means that you have some experience of it, but you either know that there's plenty of room for new ideas or you're not confident about applying what you know yet.

0 means that you've no idea whatsoever about the subject or the mere thought of having to do it fills you with terror.

Definitions:

Niche: Your specific area of coaching, your coaching expertise, the type of clients that you want to work with

Marketing message: The message that you want to communicate to prospective clients

Price: How much to charge and how to package your services

PR/publicity: How to get articles published and use the media

Public speaking: How to get booked as a public speaker and run your own workshops

Networking: How to make contacts who will introduce you to other people, word-of-mouth marketing

Internet: Using the internet to spread the word about you

Closing: Asking for the business, how to convert prospective clients into paying clients

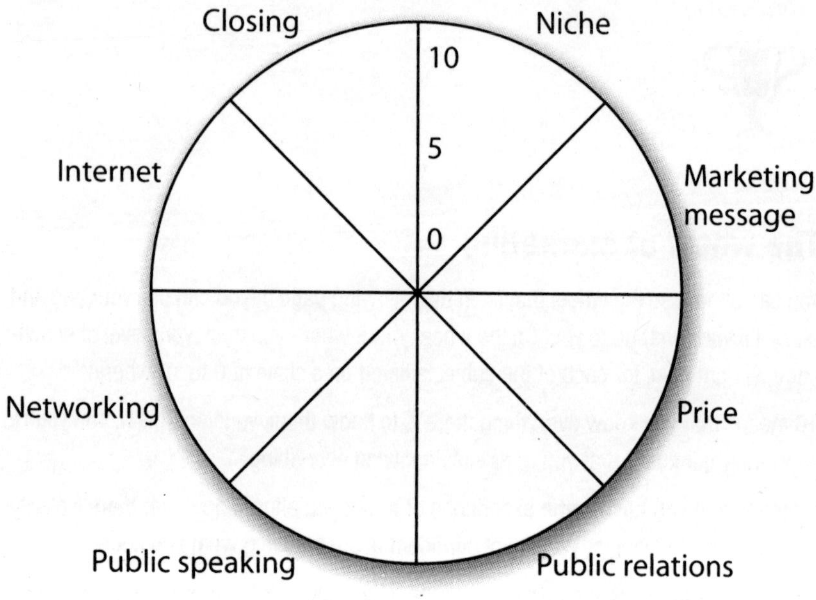

The wheel of marketing

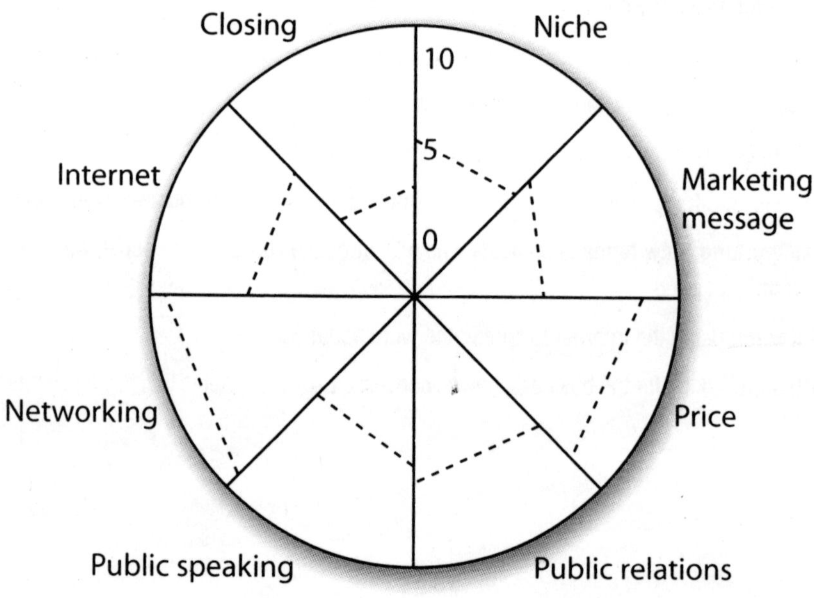

The wheel of marketing – example

How wobbly was your wheel?

It's perfectly OK if you have a wobbly wheel. After all, if you were scoring a 10 all round you probably wouldn't be reading this book!

For those areas where you scored 7 or lower, what would it take for you to improve your score? What are the things that you want to know about? What would it take for you to improve your confidence in this subject?

You'll be pleased to know that for each of the subjects on your wheel, there's a chapter dedicated to it. As you work through this book, come back to your wobbly wheel and see whether you can start to improve on your scores.

GROWing your coaching practice

Here's another coaching tool that you can use on yourself when you're starting up your coaching practice. It's also good to use it periodically throughout your coaching career to review your progress.

Let's remind ourselves of what the GROW model is all about:

G for Goal

R for Reality

O for Options; and

W for Way Forward/Will Do

When you're starting a coaching practice, you're also starting a business and, like any good business, you need to you need to have a Business Plan.

'If you fail to plan, you plan to fail'

What are your aims for your coaching practice? What do you want it to look like six months from now, a year from now, ten years from now? It's very important to plan where you're going with your practice because, if you don't, it will be very difficult to work out a strategy for getting there.

Plus, how will you know when you've got there?

When you're starting out, it's very easy to say, *"I just want to get some clients", "I need to start getting some money coming in"* or, *"I just need to start paying back the money that I've spent on the course."*

But we do need to stop and think – what are your *real* goals here? *How many* clients do you want to have? How many hours in the day are you prepared to spend coaching clients? What do you need to be bringing in on a monthly basis? How much time will you need to do the administration, and also the marketing that creates more clients?

What are the *goals* that you've set for yourself, and your coaching practice? They need to be SMART:

Specific – what *exactly* do you want?

Measurable – how can you measure your progress/achievements?

Achievable – don't set yourself up to fail, make goals achievable

Realistic – what is realistic for you and your circumstances?

Timed – when do you want to achieve your goal by?

When you do set yourself SMART goals for your practice, you are really 'walking the talk'.

EXERCISE

Using the table below (or your notepad), write down your goals for the next three months, six months and the next year. You can add some beyond that timeframe too.

	3 months	6 months	1 year
How many clients will I be working with on a monthly basis?			
How many hours a week will I spend coaching?			
How much will I be earning each month from coaching clients?			
How many hours each week will I spend on administration, marketing, accounts, etc?			

SMART goals save you money!

It is *really, really* important to have very clear goals when you're deciding on the type of marketing that you want to do. It will inform the decisions you make. For example, it's very easy to be tempted by an advertising salesperson to invest money on an advert and say, *"Okay, well that cost me £200 – I'll see what happens."*

Is your aim here to pay back that £200 or to have generated £1,000 in new business for you?

How many new enquiries do you want to generate?

How many of those people need to become clients?

If you got one new client, would that be a successful result?

And if you want to get that one client – is advertising the best way of doing it?

Are there *other* routes that could get you that one client? Which route presents the best value for your money?

Later in this book, we'll be examining your coaching niche – if you're *really specific* about the type of clients that you want to work with, it becomes an awful lot easier to *attract* them, because you understand them. You understand how they think. You understand where they search for information. You understand what their worries are – what their *concerns* are.

NLP techniques in marketing

Many coach training courses incorporate some Neuro-Linguistic Programming (NLP) techniques. May I suggest that you refer to a good NLP book as you go through this section if you have not already studied NLP. As I said in the assumptions, I have assumed that you already have at least a basic understanding of NLP techniques.

Matching and mirroring is a commonly used technique for making clients feel at ease when they are in a coaching session.

We all know that it's very important to strike up that *strong rapport* with a new client – so that they feel that they are understood, that they've been *heard*. You're their kind of person and you 'get them'. It's very important for clients to *feel* that they've been understood.

But what happens if you're not face-to-face with that client? What are the ways that you can build rapport with them?

If you're talking to them over the phone – you can start to match their tempo, their tone of voice, and the language they use by para-phrasing or using the client's words.

Marketing is rapport

When you understand the people that you want to work with and the way that they like to communicate, you can create rapport without even being engaged in a conversation with them by using your marketing.

You can adapt the language, look and style of your website, publicity materials, brochures etc to create rapport.

But it's just as easy to inadvertently break rapport through marketing. Let me give you an example:

For argument's sake, let's say that you've chosen partners in large accountancy firms as the people who you'd like to work with. You've decided to send them out a letter in a format that *you* really like.

You want to present yourself as fun and light-hearted, so it's got a bright pink header and is written in one of those hand-written fonts.

But think about how that's received at the other end. Think about the expectations of that person and how they might want to be dealt with. They consider themselves to be experienced, professional and they are used to people showing them a lot of respect. Whilst they might be fun and light-hearted themselves outside of work, they have received the letter *at work* where they are a very different person.

Whilst the content of the letter or brochure might be relevant for them, the presentation broke rapport because it didn't appear to be for 'people like them'. Would a letter in black and white in Times New Roman have worked better?

But, wait a minute, what if you sent a similar letter to parents of toddlers via their nursery telling them about parent coaching? Would that be more appropriate?

When you're designing your business cards, your website – all of the different things that are going on with your marketing – think about how you can use it to create rapport with the people who are going to be receiving it.

The better that you can understand the person that you're marketing to, the more likely it is that you'll design messages that they'll respond to well.

Modality marketing

From NLP, we know that people generally have a dominant preference for one of three main senses. There are three main representational systems and these are:

- Visual
- Auditory
- Kinesthetic

The language that people choose can give an indication of which sense they tend to use the most, for example:

- Visual – looks good to me, I see what you mean
- Auditory – sounds about right, that strikes a chord
- Kinesthetic – it hit home, gut reaction

It's fairly easy to pick up on someone's preferred sense when they are communicating directly with you, but it's not as easy when you're engaged in one-way communication, for example, writing the content for a website.

In this case, it's safer to keep your language as neutral as possible to avoid accidentally mismatching with your prospective clients.

Modeling in marketing

Modeling is the process of breaking down what it is that makes somebody successful so that it can be replicated.

You can use this process to find someone who is marketing themselves successfully and model them. Probably the most famous coach who talks about modeling is Anthony Robbins. As he says, *"Success leaves clues."*

Anthony Robbins is very successful at what he does and is known internationally but, it didn't happen overnight and you could look for clues to how he became so successful and model your approach on his.

Something that he talks about alot was how he used to read as many books on personal development as he could get his hands on. He also says that he would test and try out new techniques as soon as he learned them.

On the marketing front, here are just some of the things that he does to promote himself:

- Writes books
- Holds seminars, events and workshops
- Speaks on the TV and radio
- Writes articles
- Has a website
- Produces audio products
- Advertises on TV through infomercials
- Uses testimonials from well-known people

In addition to examining *what* he does, you can investigate *how* he does it.

Clone alert!

Have you ever heard someone say that they want to be 'the next Anthony Robbins' or 'the next Fiona Harrold'? What's wrong with being YOU, just more successful?

Please don't become a clone of someone else. You are a unique individual in the same way that Anthony Robbins and Fiona Harrold are. You can learn from them and carry that learning through to be the best 'you' possible.

Exercise

Think about a famous coach or someone you admire. What do they do to promote their services? What are the messages they use? How do they communicate with their target audience? What can you learn from them? How can you model your approach on theirs? (More later about your unique niche.)

Summary

- You already have a number of tools that you can use to plan how to attract paying clients to you
- There are seven P's in the marketing mix:
  - Product/service offering
  - Price
  - Place
  - Promotion
  - People
  - Process
  - Physical evidence
- Marketing coaching is different from marketing a product because it's intangible – your clients can't examine it before they decide to buy
- Marketing is about building rapport with prospective clients
- Use the Wheel of Marketing to track your progress
- GROW can be used to plan the development of your practice
- Set yourself SMART goals to save yourself money
- Take care to match and mirror in your marketing
- You can inadvertently mismatch with your clients through inappropriate marketing
- Use neutral language in marketing materials as you don't know which senses your clients prefer
- Model yourself on a successful coach and pay attention to *how* they market themselves

chapter two Choosing Your Niche

TWO Choosing Your Niche

Everyone talks about coaching niches. They all say you've got to have one to stand out, to attract clients and to charge a decent rate. But where do you begin? What happens if you're just starting out and you haven't coached anyone yet? Or deep down you resist the idea of excluding some clients and concentrating on coaching certain people on certain things?

Well, my aim is that by the time you've finished reading this chapter, you'll have a much better idea of how to select a niche for yourself and your coaching practice. Who knows, you might even have it sorted out in the time it takes to finish reading!

Once you're clear about your niche, all of your marketing becomes a lot easier.

Why? Because when you're clear about which clients you want to work with, it's easier to create a coherent marketing message that will actually *appeal* to people. As much as you might want to, you can't please everybody and there's no point trying.

Focus on the groups of people that are going to be more responsive to your marketing and how you can start to turn some of those into clients.

"I just want an ordinary cup of coffee"

A few years ago my husband and I went to stay with a friend who had been living in New York for some time. We asked him about how he'd found New York when he first arrived. Tired from travelling, he stumbled into a coffee shop thinking that a nice cup of coffee would perk him up. The conversation in the coffee shop went something like this:

"Good morning sir! How may I help you today?"

"Can I have a cup of coffee please?"

"Certainly, sir. Would you like a cappuccino, espresso or latte?"

"I don't know, just an ordinary cup of coffee."

"Of course. And would you like that as a decaf?"

"No, just an ordinary cup of coffee"

"With whole milk, non fat or soy?"

"I JUST WANT AN ***ORDINARY*** *CUP OF COFFEE!"*

He went into the shop with one thought in mind – to buy a cup of coffee. He had no idea that in New York there were so many options available and it eventually became overwhelming to the point where he got angry and frustrated. There must have been a part of him that wanted to shout, *"You know what? Forget the coffee I'll get something else!"*

Have you ever felt like that about choosing a coaching niche?

I have.

When I read my first book on coaching – Sir John Whitmore's *Coaching for Performance*, I was very clear about the type of coaching I wanted to do – coaching people at work to perform better in the workplace. I had corporate senior management experience and I'm a bit of a workaholic, so I would certainly have credibility and empathy with my clients if I decided to go down that route.

On my training course, my eyes were opened to the possibilities – I could coach anyone! There were so many options. Almost too many and for a number of months I dashed around trying everything, confused about what I *should* do.

It was only later that I realized that what I really wanted was that ordinary cup of coffee I'd originally gone in for. When I stopped trying to appeal to everyone and trying out all the options, and focused on what I understood and would be good at, it became much easier to attract clients.

EXERCISE

Think back to when you first thought about becoming a coach and what you wanted to do. Review your CV or resume and remind yourself what you have done well in the past. Look at your notes from the clients you have coached so far. What are your initial thoughts about the type of coaching you want to do?

There are two different ways that you can approach choosing a niche:

- The first is *Niche Coaching,* and
- The second is *Niche Marketing*

Niche coaching

Here is a short list of some of the coaching niches. I'm sure that you can think of more niches. Either jot them down at the bottom of the list or on your notepad.

Career coaching	Work/life balance coaching
Parent coaching	Spiritual coaching
Small business coaching	Fitness coaching
Weight loss coaching	Relationship coaching
Wealth coaching	Confidence coaching

More:

Let's pick just one of those coaching niches, *relationship coaching*, and think about how you might find clients looking for that type of coaching.

How would you identify and effectively market to people who might want or need to work with a relationship coach?

You could:

- Advertise in magazines
- Write for magazines and newspapers
- Advertise on the internet
- Speak at conferences and events

People who want to improve their relationships can come from all walks of life. Some will be more willing to work with a coach than others. Some will be more willing to pay for coaching than others. And some will be more willing and able to pay the rates you want to charge than others.

Niche marketing

How do you market yourself to ensure that people who are exposed to your marketing:

- Are the types of people you enjoy coaching?
- Want to be coached during the hours you want to work?
- Have the means to pay for regular coaching sessions?

This is where it is helpful to think in terms of niche marketing. Niche marketing is aiming your marketing at a specific group of people who have something in common – something more than what they might want to be coached on.

According to the Chartered Institute of Marketing, niche marketing is:

"The marketing of a product to a small and well-defined segment of the market place."

This means it's about working out who you want to attract with your marketing –what kind of *clients* do you want as opposed to what kind of *coaching* do you want to do?

Here are some groups of people you could choose to market to:

Accountants	People starting businesses
Students	Working mothers
Civil Servants	Managers seeking promotion

Etc...

Maintaining variety in your coaching practice

Both ways of niching give you a lot of variety because, if you choose say, relationship coaching – there are *all sorts* of different relationships that are out there, e.g. romantic relationships, work relationships, friendship relationships, family relationships. In addition, you could coach lots of different types of people on any one or more of those different relationships.

You've also got the variety in that if you choose a certain group of people, as we said earlier on, that all of their lifestyles are going to be very different and they may want to be coached on different things – not just relationships.

Niche coaching or niche marketing?

Personally, I find it an awful lot easier to think in terms of niche marketing first, and then think about niche coaching.

Why? Because it's much easier to start with the *kind* of people that you want to coach and then consider the challenges that they might be facing.

You can talk to your existing clients (if you want to work with more people like them) and find out what they're going through, what pressures they are under and how you would be able to work with more people like them. Your existing clients will usually be able to give you lots of information.

Of course, you could think about it the other way round if you already have a type of coaching that you're passionate about and good at. Then you can think about what types of people are most likely to want coaching on that topic or issue.

Niching online

There is an argument to say that if you want to do most of your marketing online, you have a greater chance of success by focusing on a particular kind of coaching.

This is because people would look for certain keywords like the ones below:

- Relationships
- Confidence
- Career
- Redundancy
- Parenting

However, when they visit your site, you still need to think about creating rapport with them through the language and visuals that you use.

For example, if you wanted to offer parent coaching to wealthy professionals and charge £1,000 for a coaching programme, you would need to consider how you phrase things and the images you use.

You could include statements such as:

- Have you ever heard your child call their nanny, 'Mummy'?
- Do you ever worry about whether your child will pass their entrance exams?
- How many evening meals did you eat with your child this week?
- Working late again?

Now think about the images you choose for your website. You'd need to consider whether the photos are of *people like them* – could the photos have come from their family album?

Mass marketing

I've already said that once you've identified the kind of person that you want to coach and understand their challenges, it's much easier to try and target them. This is because you can buy the mailing lists, you can get PR in the magazines that they're reading, and you can go to their networking groups.

When you understand who you're talking to, you can start to build rapport with them through your marketing.

If you watch TV commercials or listen to commercials on the radio, you'll notice that the advertisers use music, visuals and language to create rapport with the people who they're targeting. The people who are in the target group will understand and 'get' the message, and the people for whom it isn't intended will simply ignore it.

The reason is that you're exposed to so many different messages on a daily basis – it's literally in the thousands once you've counted having the radio on in the morning, opening the newspaper, driving around seeing posters, something on the back of a bus – and our minds just can't store all that information.

You have that same challenge when you're trying to grab your clients' attention. They too are exposed to so many different messages each day and they have to filter them. If your message doesn't grab them by the throat and scream, *"This is for YOU"* into their faces, the chances are they will ignore it. Relevance is absolutely *key* when you're trying to cut your way through all of the clutter.

Now we're not just talking about advertising here, we're also talking about when someone opens their e-mail inbox – it will be filled with lots of different messages. The same applies when somebody reads a magazine or reads a paper – there are lots of different articles for them to choose from.

It's the ones that seem to be really relevant and stand out to the client, or prospective client, that they are going to notice.

But you can only get that marketing spot on if you really do understand the person and the mind-set that you're talking to.

In order for your marketing to attract attention, you really must understand exactly who you want to attract.

Getting the context right

Have you ever noticed that you can be a different person when you're in different situations? For example, do you behave, speak and think in *exactly* the same way when you're with your business contacts, best friend, close family members, distant family members or partner?

Do you feel and think like the same person when you're working, exercising or relaxing?

In different contexts, we are in different frames of mind. And when we're in different frames of mind, we filter information differently. The consequence is that we also filter out marketing messages differently when we're in different contexts or settings.

This is important when you're choosing where to promote yourself. The same person could pay attention to your message in one context and completely ignore it in another.

Identifying your own niche

There are three make-or-break factors when you're choosing your niche. If you're missing one or more of them, your marketing is going to be harder than if you can find a niche where you do have all three.

They are:

- Experience,
- Credibility, and
- Contacts

Let's examine them one by one.

Experience

Experience really counts. If you can demonstrate to prospective clients that you have helped people like them facing similar situations before, it's a lot easier for them to believe that you can do the same for them.

Questions to ask:

- Have I coached people like this before?
- Can I demonstrate that I've got good results for people in similar situations before? (e.g. testimonials)
- How confident am I that I can effectively handle any issues that might come up in the coaching session?
- Where do I have experience?
- If I don't have experience, how can I get some?
- Who do I understand?

Credibility

In order to win clients, it's important to be taken seriously by them. By that I mean that you are credible and they have respect for you and your abilities. Credibility comes from being recognized as someone who knows what they're talking about.

Questions to ask:

- Where/with whom to I currently have credibility?
- Do I have the necessary qualifications to coach?
- Are there any other qualifications or memberships I could have that would help them to take me seriously?
- If the coaching is work-related, have I worked in their field before or worked with people like them as clients in another capacity, e.g. as a consultant or trainer?
- Can I speak their language – do I understand their jargon and short-hand?
- Do I look, sound and act the part?
- Can I empathize with them?
- Have I written a book or had articles published on this topic?
- Do I do any public speaking on this subject/to these people?
- If I don't think people would take me seriously right now, what can I do to build my profile?
- Do I walk the talk?*

* Ideally, a coach should be a living example of how things can be different for their client, for example:

- If you are unhealthy and over-weight and want to coach on weight-loss or fitness, you may find it difficult to be taken seriously by prospective clients
- If you have a string of failed relationships behind you, clients may question your ability to coach on relationships – unless of course, you've finally found 'the one' and you're blissfully happy

Contacts

Ask most established coaches and they'll tell you that they get the majority of their new clients through word-of-mouth and recommendations. How can you do this if no one knows who you are?

Questions to ask:

- Who do I already know in this niche?
- What niches do I already have contacts in?
- Who would be willing to give me a testimonial and recommend me to other people?
- Who can I take for coffee/lunch to pick their brains?
- How can I get myself in front of as many prospective clients as possible?
- Where can I network with my prospective clients?

Don't panic!

If you're missing one of the areas above, you can still coach in the niche, but accept that it will take a little longer to find clients. The Venn Diagram on the next page shows you what to do if you're missing an essential element.

Ideally, you want to be operating in the central area, where all three circles overlap, i.e. you have experience, credibility and contacts.

The next step

Before you start doing your marketing, there are three questions that you need to ask of any target group or niche:

1. Do they have a problem?
2. Are they willing to pay to fix it?
3. Are they part of a group that I can market to?

If you can answer YES to ALL of these questions, then you're on your way!

Prospective clients usually have something in their lives that they would like to change – after all, if their life was exactly as they wanted it to be, they wouldn't need a coach! For you to make a living as a coach, you need to focus your attention on clients who would like to change something and are willing to pay for coaching.

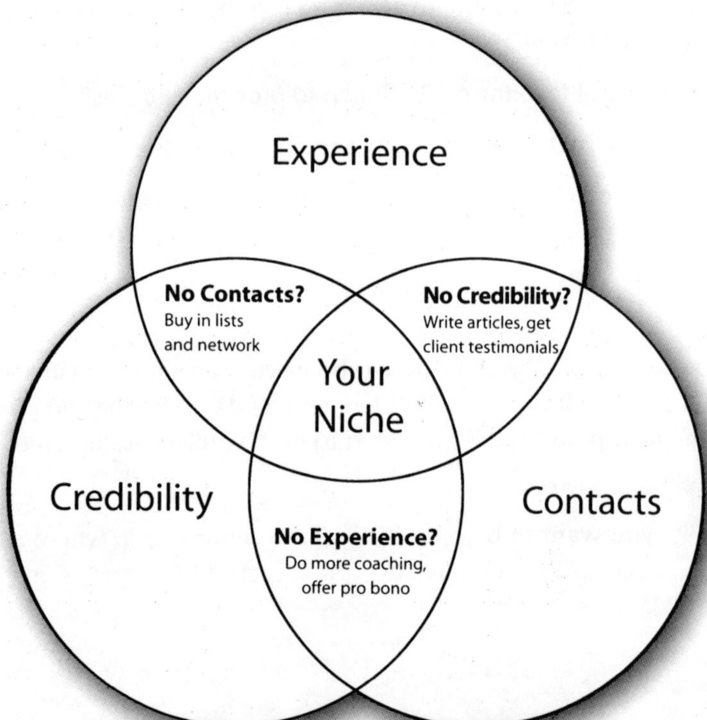

© Hannah McNamara

Unfortunately, many coaches try to market to groups who, whilst they might desperately want coaching, either aren't able to afford coaching or aren't prepared to pay for it. For example, people who are facing redundancy could get a lot of benefit from sessions with a coach, but if they don't know when they'll have a regular income again, there's a chance that they may cut back spending to the bare essentials unless they have had a substantial pay-out or their employer will pay for coaching. Coaching may not feature in their list of bare essentials.

Finally, for your marketing to be effective (and cost-effective), you must be able to market to these clients as part of a group.

For example, lots of people struggle with work/life balance.

- How do you market to people with this issue?
- Is it easier to think about which types of people have particular challenges surrounding work/life balance?
- Which jobs or professions demand long hours in the office or require employees to work shifts or to be on call?
- How would you market to people working in these particular jobs or professions?

EXERCISE – WHAT ARE YOUR TARGET CLIENTS LIKE?

Some of these questions will be relevant to your target clients, some will not, but fill in as many as you can because it will help you to build up a clearer picture of who you are targeting, and make it easier for you to contact them.

Ask yourself the following questions about people in your niche:

1. What problem keeps your client awake at night? For example, trying to think of a new career, troubled relationships, having to make a speech

2. Are they willing to pay to fix it? Will they pay what you want to charge? (The person paying the bill is the client and may not be the coachee so they must be willing to pay for someone else to have coaching.)
3 How can you market to them as a group? For example, do they read the same trade magazine, can you buy a mailing list, do they belong to a club or association?

The best-kept secret about niches

As your practice develops, you can coach in more than one niche. For one thing, it keeps life interesting – you don't keep coaching on the same issues all the time. For another, it means that you can work with a range of clients, with a range of fee-structures. You could have one niche that pays the bills and keeps you in caviar and diamonds, e.g. executive coaching for high-flying professionals at £200/hr, and one niche that you coach because you want to make a difference to people who otherwise couldn't afford you, e.g. parent coaching for single parents relying on benefits at £20/hr or even free. You don't have to charge the same amounts for everyone – just make sure that you keep the marketing to each niche separate, perhaps with different brochures or websites. And even consider having a different logo for each.

Summary

- Faced with a lot of choice, it can be confusing choosing a niche
- There is a difference between niche coaching and niche marketing
- Niche coaching is about the type of coaching you do and the topic you coach on
- Niche marketing is about the type of people you coach
- People can ignore your messages if they receive them in the wrong context
- When choosing a niche, pick one where you have experience, credibility and contacts
- You can choose more than one niche to market to

chapter three **Positioning**

THREE Positioning

This chapter is all about how you position yourself in the market place and how you want your clients to think of you.

There are seven main areas to think about when it comes to deciding how to position yourself.

1. Target market

Before you think about how you're going to position yourself in the market, think about who are you trying to attract. *I know* we've already talked about this, but unless you really understand your clients and design your marketing specifically for them, you'll try to appeal to everyone and end up appealing to no-one.

There are two main ways of classifying your clients:

- Demographics, or
- Psychographics

Demographics includes:

- How old are your clients?
- What sort of job do they do?
- Do they run a business?
- What sort of income bracket are they in?

Psychographics is slightly different. This is more about their mind-set:

- What life stage are they in?
- What interests do they have?
- What are their attitudes towards certain things?

For example, it may be that you want to attract the kind of person that would take time out to go to a retreat. That could include someone who's eighteen and someone who's eighty. They could come from lots of different backgrounds with very different life experiences but what they *do* have in common is their attitude towards life and themselves.

2. Your offering

Your offering as a coach – is it only going to be one-to-one coaching? But even if it is one-to-one coaching, how are you breaking that down?

Are you positioning yourself as someone who does:

- Face-to-face?
- Telephone?
- Both?

Would you also think about running tele-classes? Doing group workshops? Would you like to have a product like a book or CD out there? Now the fantastic thing about a product is that you can package up:

- Your years of experience
- Your coaching questions
- Your exercises – the tools that you've come up with as a coach

And you can package them in a way that's affordable to your client and allows you to coach multiple clients at once.

While you're busy doing a one-to-one session with somebody else – or even while you're asleep or while you're walking the dogs – you can have somebody who's:

- Listening to your CD
- Reading your book
- Downloading your e-book
- Downloading your report
- Taking part in online exercises
- Contributing to your online forums

What if these things can be going on while you're doing something else? It would allow you as a coach to serve more people.

One of the frustrations that I hear from coaches is that there are only so many hours in the day. They want to work with lots of people, they want to be able to make a difference.

Having a range of products at a range of different price points allows you to serve more people and, of course, it also allows you to have a passive income as well.

At some point, the time will come when you want to step away from one-to-one coaching, or you want to cut down your hours. Something happens, something changes in your life and you're not able to put the same amount of hours in.

Or, you've started coaching at such a level where you're becoming too expensive for a lot of your prospective clients. Or you're in so much demand that you can pick and choose who you have as clients, you can choose what to charge.

Having products for clients to buy allows you to have a residual income, and still allow people to benefit from your experience without engaging you as their coach.

3. The experience

I don't mean your experience as a coach. What I mean is the *client's* experience. We've already talked about coaching being an intangible thing and it's difficult for the client to judge whether it will work for them before they've committed to becoming a client.

You can position yourself based on the actual experience that the client has when they come to you.

It can be helpful to think about:

- What is the service that you'll offer?
- What are your quality standards that you want to put in place?
- Do you want to make sure that if a client e-mails you, you'll respond within twenty-four hours?
- If a client leaves a message for you, how quickly will you respond to them?
- If in a coaching session you say you're going to send something out to your client, for example a piece of homework, how quickly will you do so?

- What are the standards for yourself and your coaching practice?
- What is the service level like?
- What are you prepared to do to make sure they get the kind of results that they want?

4. Competition

As a coach, you have *direct competition* and *indirect competition.*

Direct compctition the other coaches in your area operating in your niche. How do you position yourself against them? Are you the person:

- Who has been there, done that and worn the T-shirt?
- Are you the person who really understands?

Are you positioned slightly differently from the other coaches:

- Becausc you'vc published a book?
- Because you're a public speaker?
- Because you're in demand?

How else can you position yourself to that you're slightly different from the other coaches that might bc in direct competition with you?

But competition doesn't just have to come from other coaches, it can be from the whole personal development field!

Indirect Competition – this is less obvious and includes your client's:

- Friends
- Family
- GP
- Personal trainer

EXERCISE

Get out your pad and think about who else your prospective clients might turn to for help and support. Ask yourself how you would position yourself against them. How are your services similar/different to theirs?

Thinking about your competitors – are they *really* competitors or could you work together and refer clients between you?

5. Five year business plan – Who do you want to be?

As coaches, we understand the benefits of having goals, but I often find that coaches themselves are reluctant to write down their goals in the form of a business plan.

Why could this be? Well, many coaches value freedom, choice and flexibility. As a result, the very act of writing a structured plan and sticking to it goes against their values. On some level, coaches can get the sense that they aren't honouring their values of freedom, choice and flexibility if they have a business plan.

Others will take the view that 'what will be will be' or 'the universe will provide' or even that some greater being has already mapped out their life/business plan for them. It's nice of them to do your business plan for you, isn't it? Would it be too much trouble for them to share it with you?

Let me ask you this: how much do you value honesty and integrity? If they feature on your list of values, then to honour those values, you need to 'walk your talk'. And if you're stressing the importance of having written goals when you're working with your clients, you'd better make sure that you have a business plan of your own. The universe *will* provide for you – provided you tell it what you want!

One of the greatest challenges when you're starting or re-inventing a business is that it can be difficult to predict what's going to happen next week, let alone next month or next year. It's understandable that many people resist this process, unless of course they are forced to do a business plan in order to get a bank loan.

So I'm going to let you off the hook to a certain extent.

Your five-year plan doesn't just have to be about how you're going to build up your coaching practice, how many clients you'll have and how much money you'll take each month. It could be the different phases that your coaching practice will go through and when.

Let me explain. If you're fresh out of training, you need experience fast. Without experience it can be hard to attract the higher paying clients, for example corporate contracts because you're an unknown quantity and you have very little physical evidence that you're any good.

There are three main phases that your coaching practice will go through:

- Pre-launch
- Launch
- Maturity

Pre-launch

This is where you're making connections and getting as many clients as possible to help you gain experience and testimonials.

You might consider offering coaching at a lower rate to make it more accessible to more people and allow you to build up your client base quickly – it takes longer to find a large quantity of people willing to pay £100 than it does to find people willing to pay £35 for a session. You can coach lots of different people and find out what type of clients you enjoy working with, and the topics you enjoy coaching on.

For example, you could say to people, *"I've just qualified as a coach and I'll be launching my coaching practice in three months time, when I'll be charging £55 per hour (or whatever you decide to charge). Until then, I'm keen to build up my client list and so for any clients who go ahead with coaching sessions before then they will be charged £35."*

This way your clients know that:

- You're still gaining experience
- The price will increase soon, so they'd better get in quick
- They can be involved in helping someone get started

What's in it for you?

- You get clients to work with and learn from
- Because they know you're still gaining experience, you can more easily ask for their feedback
- You can test different techniques and formats with them
- You gain confidence

When you start to get busier and your confidence builds it's time to increase your rates and move to the *launch phase*.

Launch

The launch phase is when you are doing lots of activities designed to spread the word and attract clients who pay your regular rate. This phase can last for a year or two while you build up a reputation and a name for yourself.

You'll have made some decisions on the type of people you want to work with and your marketing will be geared towards them. Much of your marketing will be designed to increase your exposure.

When you enter this phase, you may be trading under your own name or have a company name. People who work with you for the first time are more likely to have responded to your marketing than have been referred by someone else, so you still need to help them to understand who you are, what you do and why your rates are set at that level.

Maturity

The maturity phase is when you have built yourself a solid reputation and most of your new clients come through word of mouth recommendations and referrals. When clients in your niche think about working with a coach, it's your name that they think of first.

In this phase, you may have a waiting list of clients who want to work with you or you might have associate coaches who you refer over-flow work to. You may still be trading under your own name, but you may also have formed a limited company and use a company name.

Price becomes less of an issue, because new clients have been recommended to you by existing/past clients and they understand that if they want to work with *you* – the specialist in this area, they have to pay a bit more than if they went to someone else.

It's more likely that coaches who are in this phase will be given the opportunity to work on larger, corporate contracts because those coaches have a proven track-record and relevant experience. They are also more confident about coaching in challenging circumstances. There will be times when they are asked to work with people who are cynical about coaching because the coachee has been *allocated* a coach rather than having *asked* for one, and they are able to deal with the situation well and explain coaching in terms that make sense to them.

So there are the three phases and your positioning in the market will depend on which phase you're in.

You might start off doing personal coaching and then when your experience and confidence increases, you might like to move into the corporate sector or coach small business owners.

Your five-year plan can include these phases and you may decide to have a different brand or identity during each phase.

6. Your brand

Your brand is not a logo or a name. It's what you stand for and the experience that clients have when they come to you. The logo or name is there to reinforce the brand and help people to identify with you.

This is where your personal values come in. Who are you as a person? What do you stand for? How are you different from other people?

Lots of people have the same values: honesty, integrity, trust.

Clients will take these as a given. They expect you to be honest, have integrity and that they can trust you, because if you don't have those values, you probably shouldn't be coaching.

What are the brand values and attributes that make you different? Here are a few that might trigger some thoughts – you can come up with more I'm sure:

Professional	Out-going	Irreverent
Gentle	Detailed	Down-to-earth
Larger-than-life	Traditional	Innovative

Once you have a list of words that describe you and the experience that you offer to your clients, it's much easier to ensure that, in everything you do, you live up to your brand.

For example, if one of your brand values is that you're innovative, would it be right for you to run your coaching practice in exactly the same way as everyone else and for your website to look like any other coach's website?

As an innovative coach, you'd present things in a fresh way and keep abreast of new techniques and models and actively use them whenever appropriate with your clients.

The name and logo that you choose for your coaching practice should reflect your brand values so that people 'get it' when they see it.

You know you've got your branding right when you show it to someone and they 'get' what you're about just by looking at it. If you want to look innovative – look innovative. If you want to look professional – look professional. And so on.

There are also ways that you can use *other people's* brands to help you to get clients.

If having your own brand isn't as important to you as working as a coach with interesting clients, talk to other coaches who are in your field and share the same values, then find out whether you can join them as an associate coach – operating under their brand. You'll be an extension of them and their company.

When you work as an associate, the person referring the work to you will probably take a commission – but you'd expect them to. If they are out there doing all the marketing for you, and all you have to do is turn up and coach the client, it's perfect! Everybody wins. In this way, you can use other people's brands to help you to get some work.

There is also the option of running a coaching franchise. Being part of a franchise operation means that they have already developed the branding, the services and there is a certain level of goodwill attached to their name.

You could think about aligning yourself with training companies. Many trainers just love to train and they may want someone else to offer coaching as a follow-up to the training courses.

Other people's brands can be used in terms of testimonials – can you get somebody who is very well-known to give you a testimonial? Is it worth you coaching them for *free* to get it?

Consider whether there are people you know who have mailing lists. You could ask whether you would be able to send a message out to people on their list – take advantage of their *brand*, even if their brand is *their name*. Sending something out to their clients in a mailing that is from them gives you a kind of endorsement. Take care to align yourself with the kinds of people who have similar brand values to your own, so that you position yourself correctly.

7. The barriers to brand success

There are four barriers that could halt the success of your brand and your coaching practice:

i) Insufficient awareness to generate trial

If no-one knows you're there – nobody will try you out.

ii) Not living the brand

If you want to be positioned as the professional coach – are you professional in *everything* that you do? If you want to be positioned as the *fun* coach – are you *fun*, when somebody calls you at eight o'clock in the morning (8am)? Are you *fun* when you turn up at a networking event? Or are you grumbling in a corner somewhere? Make sure that you live your brand.

iii) Standing out in ways that the client doesn't care about

Yes, you've put a lot of time and effort into doing all of your training courses. Yes, you've added lots of other skills, but when you meet that prospective client:

- Do they care how many certificates you've got?
- Do they care who you trained with?

Or

- Do they care about whether you can get them the results that they want?

Yes, training is very important – and I'm not saying that it isn't important. But what I'm saying is if you position yourself on being the best *qualified* coach in the marketplace – you're going to be positioning yourself as the best *academic* coach and not necessarily the best coach in a *practical* sense.

iv) Insufficient margin or keeping your costs too high

This means not charging enough to make a profit, or keeping your costs too high.

There is no point being the £200 an hour coach if nobody hires you! Equally, there's no point charging £60 per hour for face-to-face coaching if it costs you £40 to hire the meeting room to coach them in, plus £5 for you to park your car.

Consider your costs and what your clients are prepared to pay. You must at least cover the costs associated with running your coaching practice if you are going to make *any* money as a coach.

Summary

There are seven areas to think about when positioning yourself in the market:

1. Target market – who are you trying to appeal to?
2. Your offering – what exactly are you offering?
3. The experience – what standards will you have?
4. Competition – who are your direct and indirect competitors? Can you work together with any of them?
5. Five-year business plan – there are three phases:
    a. Pre-launch,
    b. Launch and
    c. Maturity
6. Your brand – it's more than a logo or a name, it's who you are and what you stand for
7. The barriers to brand success – there are four:
    a. Insufficient awareness to generate trial
    b. Not living the brand
    c. Standing out in areas that the client doesn't care about
    d. Insufficient margin or keeping your costs too high

chapter four **Pricing**

FOUR Pricing

This chapter examines how to set your prices and position yourself in the market place.

Very few coaches discuss their rates openly or publish them on their websites or brochures. Not only does this make it difficult for clients to know how much coaching usually costs, but it makes it hard for new coaches to understand what the 'going rate' is and how to set their coaching fees.

The result is that many new coaches either under-price themselves or set their rates much higher than other coaches with similar levels of experience/ expertise. In both cases, this can mean that they struggle to find the 'right' clients because they are either perceived as:

- Too cheap – *"they can't be any good"*
- Too expensive – *"they are ripping people off"*

Generally, this is because many new coaches don't have access to information about what other coaches are *actually* charging, as opposed to what people might *tell* them that they are charging.

Remember that whilst someone quotes their day rate for large organizations at £2,000, in reality they may only have a few days booked at that rate each year. They may spend most of their time coaching personal clients at £60 per hour.

There are a number of surveys and studies on what coaches are actually charging and some of them are quoted in this chapter. You can find up-to-date information by searching on the internet.

Your guilty secret...

This may or may not apply to you, but some coaches actually feel guilty about charging their coaching clients. This could be for a number of reasons:

- *"The client does all the work to achieve their goals, I'm just the facilitator."*
- *"I want to coach everyone."*
- *"I love coaching and feel guilty charging for doing something that I love."*
- *"They probably can't afford the rates I want to charge."*
- *"I've never had to ask anyone for money before and I don't want to."*
- *"This is my purpose in life."*
- *"I don't think I'm worth it."*

It's beyond the scope of this book to coach you on any guilty feelings and limiting beliefs about money, but I will just make a few points now and then we'll move on to how much people are charging.

OK. If your clients *could* do it on their own they would have done so already and they wouldn't need a coach. Just because the client is the one doing all the work and setting the goals, doesn't mean that you don't exist and you didn't make a significant contribution to their success. You did and you deserve to be rewarded for what you have done for them

How much time have you invested in honing your coaching skills? Weeks? Months? Years? However long it took, that represents time away from your friends, your family and your hobbies. How much is that time worth? You have invested in your professional qualifications and developing your abilities – are you trying to tell me that that investment was worthless?

As for feeling guilty for charging for doing something you love, do you think Madonna feels guilty for getting paid to perform in front of packed stadiums? Does David Beckham give himself six lashes each time he plays a football match?

If it crosses your mind that what they do is somehow 'different' from what you do, think again. How many people has Madonna inspired to follow their dreams and shout *"I'm going to be successful, no matter what you say"*? And what about the boys and girls who, right now, are pushing themselves to train that bit harder because they aspire to being as successful as David Beckham?

What about the 'feel-good factor'? Each of these people has the ability to lift someone's day, whether it's by singing along or getting excited about a match. You are in a position where you can make an even more dramatic difference to your client's lives. What do you think that is worth to them?

As for assuming that other people won't pay what you want to charge, is this because *you* couldn't afford to pay what you're charging? Seriously, you could be sabotaging your own success through this limiting belief. If I can make a suggestion, work with your own coach on this so that you don't hold yourself back.

A boss of mine always used to say, "Fish where there are fish". What he meant by that was dangle your rod where you're more likely to get a bite. Promote yourself to people who are likely to become your clients and stop fishing where there are no fish – it's a waste of time and can destroy your confidence.

Some coaches have said to me, *"My friends say I'm charging too much and that I should get a* **proper job.***"* I'm sorry to be harsh about this, but are your friends your target market? They may not have a clue about how much the average rates are for coaching and could be comparing your rates to having their tarot cards read or getting a pedicure.

There will always be people who have vested interest in you not succeeding. These are the people whose role in life is to be there for you when you're sobbing on the phone or to give you a cuddle and say, *"Life's a bitch, isn't it?"* To see you changing and taking brave moves that secretly they might have wanted to make themselves but were too scared to, is unsettling for them. It threatens their position in the world. After all, what would happen to them if you didn't need a shoulder to cry on? They'd be redundant.

Do you believe that coaching works? If you do, then you know what it's worth and that you deserve to make a living from it.

Maslow's hierarchy of needs

Maslow stated that people have different needs ranging from having food in their bellies to feeling that they are contributing to society. The needs were illustrated as a pyramid with the basic needs at the bottom. The basic needs must be satisfied before those above. I've found that if people try to satisfy the higher needs before the basic needs, there is inner conflict and an underlying feeling of panic. Clients can pick up on this desperation and it can make them feel uncomfortable about working with you unless you manage it carefully.

As a coach, it's important for you to understand where you are on the pyramid and which is the next stage for you. It's not surprising that if you don't have enough money for food, you'll struggle to feel comfortable coaching people for free on a regular basis.

Here's an illustration of Maslow's hierarchy of needs, with my own interpretations.

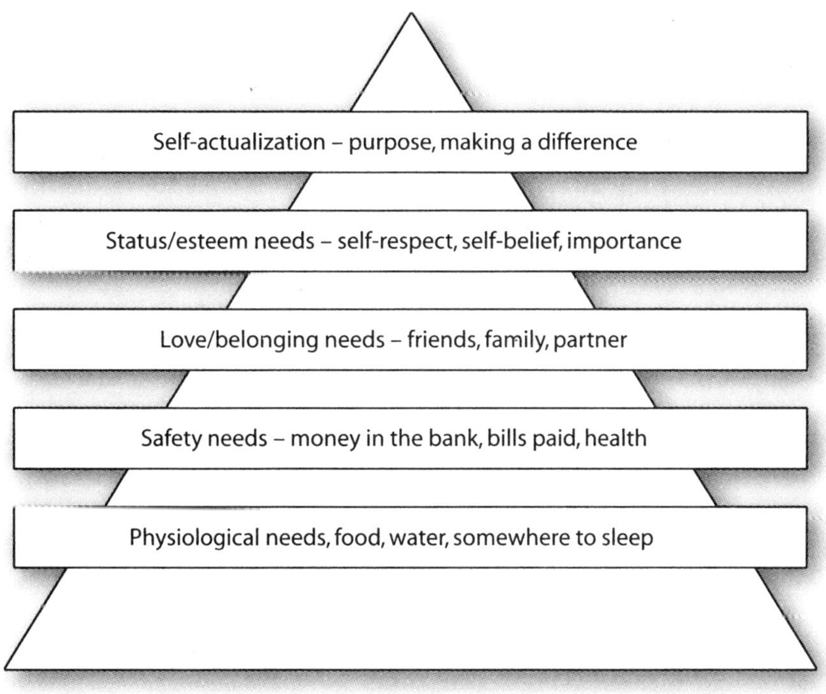

Here's another little secret...

Many coaches have part-time jobs or even full-time jobs whilst they build up a client base. There's a myth that everyone completes their qualification, gives up their job and immediately has a thriving coaching practice paying them double their previous salary.

Personally, I worked part-time in a furniture shop for a few months to bring some money in and keep the wolves from the door. This worked out really well for me because the shop wasn't very busy during the week and my boss said that it was absolutely fine for me to use the computer for my own business and take calls on my mobile, provided that if there were customers in the shop, they came first.

In the time I was alone in the shop (which was most days!) I listened to CDs on coaching, sales techniques and negotiating, and I read books on personal development and setting up a business. I also decided that rather than driving to work and paying to park my car all day, I'd get the bus there and use the journey time to listen to CDs and read. While I was in the shop, I was getting paid to learn!

The best part was that when customers did come into the shop, I got to try out the sales and negotiating techniques I'd just learned about.

Failure is not an option!

I'd like to make something very clear: you have **not** failed if your coaching practice is not profitable immediately. Should you decide to take a part-time job, you have **not** failed, you have simply taken control of the situation and done something about it. You have been proactive. Provided you are determined to push yourself and you believe in yourself and your abilities, you will succeed in time. Have a clear goal and take the necessary steps to achieving that goal.

International Coach Federation (ICF) survey

In 2004 a survey by the ICF was published in *The International Journal of Evidence Based Coaching and Mentoring.*[1] It's a very interesting study and worth looking at a copy yourself online.

Approximately 2,500 coaches responded to this survey. The majority of them were in the United States, with the remainder from mainly English speaking countries such as Canada, UK and Australia.

I'm writing this in the UK in 2006, so given that the US market for coaching is probably around five years ahead of the UK market, it gives UK coaches an indication of coming trends.

One of the things they looked at was how much coaches were earning on average:

- 52.5% were earning under $30,000 per year (approx £17,000)
- 32.3% were earning under $10,000 per year (approx £5,500)

This may seem startling when everyone around you is telling you that the demand for coaching is growing and you can earn good money as a coach, especially if you have no other source of income and have bills to pay. It's worth noting that almost half of the respondents reported that their coaching businesses had been established for less than two years, so many of them had yet to build up their practice fully.

They also surveyed the amount of time that people were spending coaching clients:

- 31.9% spent 5-10 hours coaching per week
- 34.5% spent more than 10 hours coaching per week
- 33.5% spent less than 5 hours coaching per week

The average seems to be that people were spending between five and ten hours coaching per week. That could be a couple of hours each day coaching or two/three days coaching, with the rest of the time on their own personal development, learning new techniques, administration, marketing and other functions.

---

1. Volume Two, Number Two, Autumn 2004 Report: Executive, Workplace and Life Coaching – Findings from a large scale survey of International Coach Federation's Members

While we're on the subject, it's important for you to set aside time for your own personal development and updating your skills. This is particularly important if you are coaching in the workplace where you may be expected to keep abreast of new management tools and any changes that could impact on your clients. If you are operating in another niche area of coaching, for example parent coaching, keep yourself informed of new TV shows, articles in the press and any related books on the best-sellers list, because your clients will be watching/reading them and will expect you to know about them.

If you choose to coach people who work in a particular trade or profession, then it's a good idea to subscribe to the specialist magazines and newspapers catering for them. Reading them for three months should give you a good understanding of current issues and help you to understand your clients' perspective on things. This is also useful if there are articles that support coaching because you can refer to them in your marketing literature, or you could even offer to be a contributor to the magazine or newspaper.

Reading around your subject or your niche area of coaching is useful because there may be situations where a client asks you for advice. Rather than frustrate them by saying that it's not your job as a coach to give advice, you could recommend a book to them that covers the subject in more detail.

For example, *Who Moved My Cheese?* by Dr. Spencer Johnson is good for clients who are experiencing uncomfortable changes and, another of his best-sellers, co-written with Kenneth Blanchard, *The One Minute Manager* is good for people who want tips on managing other people.

How do coaches market themselves?

The ICF survey asked respondents about what type of coaching they were doing. The vast majority (97.4%) stated that they did one-to-one coaching, no surprises there!

These are the other activities that coaches were doing:

- 63.4% of the respondents were doing seminars and workshops
- 52.1% were doing public speaking, and
- 48.2% were doing group coaching

All of the above activities are fantastic ways to demonstrate to a group of people exactly what you can do for them. It allows you to build up trust and credibility with them by allowing them to experience what you're like to work with, before committing to one-to-one coaching.

It's a lot easier for somebody to go to a workshop or see you speak at an event and *then* hire you as their coach – rather than it is for them to take a chance and commit to one-to-one coaching with you. You're an unknown quantity at that stage and it can give them faith in your ability to help them if they can see you work in another environment first.

How long does it take to start building a practice?

According to the ICF survey, 52.1% of respondents had ten paying clients in under twelve months, typically within six to twelve months (27.4%). Of the people that were surveyed 26.2% had not yet had ten clients.

Does this mean there are a lot of coaches out there who aren't getting much business? Yes.

With this type of survey it tends to be the people who are new to the market and new to the profession who will respond because they want to know what else is going on out there in the big wide world; so it can skew things slightly.

But there will be people who have not yet had ten clients and *may never* get more than ten clients. It all depends on how committed you are to promoting yourself as a coach and the contacts and connections that you already have. Generally this survey indicates that it's going to take between six and twelve months to really get going from a standing start. If you already have a business or a book of clients and you're adding coaching to your portfolio of services, then you could start working with coaching clients much faster.

How do coaches price their services?

Like other professionals, we have become used to setting our prices by the hour. However, the trend in the US appears to be to charge on a monthly basis, not an hourly basis.

The ICF showed that 58.8% of the coaches surveyed, priced on a monthly basis. Why could this be? Let's think about this from the client's perspective:

> Client: "I'm interested in some coaching, how much do you charge?"
>
> Coach: "My fees are £80 per hour."
>
> Client: "How many hours will I need?"
>
> Coach: "It depends on what you want to achieve. I have packages available for 6 and 12 sessions..."

When the client asks, *"How many hours will I need?"* what they're really asking is, *"How much is it actually going to cost me in total?"* They need to make a decision based on how much they can afford to spend, which will depend on their level of disposable income. No matter how much they need the coaching, if a client has to decide between paying the mortgage and paying your fees, the mortgage will usually come first.

Even when a client presents you with a relatively straight-forward goal, for example to perform better in job interviews, once the coaching begins they may want to explore other issues that take longer to work through.

When a client comes to you initially, you really don't know how long it will take for them to make the changes that they want to, so it's difficult for you to give them a definite price because at that stage you really don't know. You can talk to them about your usual packages – but in terms of how many sessions, well it's as long as a piece of string because who knows?

What else can happen is that, particularly for people who are watching a budget, they'll worry that you'll extend things and you'll add in extra sessions when they don't need them.

If you have ever bought a house, gone through a divorce, or anything that's involved using a professional who charges by the hour, it's natural to think about the number of letters being sent and the phone calls made because you're being charged according to the time they spend on them. People can suspect that if you're charging by the hour, you'll stretch it out to as many hours as possible. Now, I know that you wouldn't do that, but remember, the client hasn't worked with you before and you need to gain their trust.

The other draw-back in charging by the hour is that you can't take time off without losing money. What happens when you want to take a holiday, you're sick or you need to take time out to care for someone else, for example children or elderly relatives?

So how do you get away from the hourly pricing trap? Well, you could consider charging on a monthly basis. It suits business clients particularly well because they like to budget, they like to think about their cash flow. But it can also suit your personal clients very well too.

Then it's just a matter of having a rolling contract with them they know how much to budget because most people are paid on a monthly basis.

Another option is to charge a fixed fee for helping someone to achieve a particular goal. This may interest business clients who are attracted by the equivalent of a 'no win, no fee' contract. However, please do take care when offering this on a coaching contract as (unless this is part of the arrangement) you are not in a consultancy role where you can be more prescriptive about what the client needs to do to get results. Ultimately it is the client who takes responsibility for making things happen and you shouldn't put your fee at risk by working with people who may not follow through on their agreed actions and fail to achieve their goals.

What is coaching worth to the client?

At any point when you're talking about pricing, it's very important to think about how much the coaching is *worth* to the client – not just how much it costs. For example:

- How much is it worth for a client to patch up a relationship with somebody they haven't spoken with for years?
- How much is it worth to them to get a promotion that gets them a £10,000 pay rise?
- How much is it worth to have the satisfaction of standing up to that person who's been bullying them?

A few hundred pounds for coaching is small in comparison. It can be a really good investment for them because the rewards, both financially and in their quality of life can be worth much, much more than the money they initially spent.

How much do coaches actually charge?

For ease, the surveys I've looked at asked coaches to quote their hourly rates. Some studies (ICF, Association for Coaching[2]) quoted an hourly rate of between £55 (approx. $100) and £85 (approx. $149), with the average for the UK being £60-£75 for personal coaching.

Rates for corporate and executive coaching in larger organizations can range from £170 (approx. $300) to £250 (approx. $500) per hour.

Of course there will be people charging much more and people charging much less.

It depends on a number of factors including:

- The services that you're offering
- Whether you offer packages/monthly rates
- What the market will tolerate
- Geographical location
- Type of coaching offered
- The coach's experience and expertise
- The coach's 'personal brand'

The survey conducted by the Association for Coaching came up with some interesting results. Coaches who responded to the survey reported that their individual session rate was between £50 and £75 per hour.

However, it tended to be over £100 per session per hour when included as part of a package or monthly rate.

Do you think that's strange? Wouldn't you have thought that a package or monthly rate would be cheaper for the client?

So, why can you charge more when it's part of a package?

Because you can bundle in lots of other services that you *can't* when you're charging by the hour.

---

2 Association for Coaching, Summary Report: UK Coaching Rates, October 2004

It creates a win-win scenario for both the coach and the client because:

- They have access to a greater level of service
- You have a regular income that you can predict

What can you include in coaching packages?

There are lots of 'extras' that you can offer to your clients when they are paying a monthly rate.

- Unlimited e-mail coaching – they can send you an e-mail between sessions and you guarantee to respond within 24 or 48 hours
- Access to a members-only area of your website where they can download exercises, articles and other resources
- Subscription to your newsletter
- Access to recordings of workshops or tele-classes you've run
- Emergency laser coaching – a 10 minute quick coaching call in emergency situations or before important meetings

Now you might say, *"What happens if I bundle in unlimited e-mail coaching and they stuff my inbox full of messages or I give them the option to call me at a moments notice if say, they've got an emergency Sales Meeting they need to go into – won't I end up being* ***used****?"*

Well, in a word – No.

It's incredibly unlikely that people will take advantage of you if you've got a working relationship built on mutual trust and respect.

I've offered these services to most of my clients and even though a lot of them have my home phone number and personal mobile number, I very, very rarely get calls on them.

People do make use of the unlimited e-mail coaching option, but usually they use it to share successes with me or to ask questions such as 'Do you know anyone who can design me a good website?' and I'm able to respond at a time that fits in with my coaching schedule.

How much should I charge?

When you're setting your own coaching rates, first think in terms of how much you want to earn on an annual or monthly basis.

Look back at the SMART goals you set for yourself in Chapter 1. Thinking about how much you'd like to have earned a year from now, let's do some calculations.

Let's say you need to have earned a minimum of £17,000 net – that's the amount that you have in your pocket to pay your personal bills, after tax.

It's time to get out your calculator and work out for yourself:

- How many hours a week do you want to spend coaching?
- How much will you charge per session/per month?
- How many sessions will you need to have booked in?

This gives you your *income*.

For argument's sake, let's say that you'll be charging £60 per hour, so you'll need to do about 285 hours of coaching each year. That's 5 or 6 hours of coaching per week or one client appointment per working day.

Goodness gracious me! (Or other exclamations that I can't print here!)

At that hourly rate, you could work full-time (40 hours) and earn a staggering £124,800 each year! No wonder people say that there's a lot of money to be made from coaching!

Wait! Before you get carried away, remember that unless you have staff to do everything else for you, there will be certain necessary activities that will take up your time that you probably won't be able to earn money directly from.

These include:

- Writing up and reviewing client notes
- Preparation between sessions
- Marketing, including time at networking events
- Writing articles or books

- Giving presentations and talks to advertise your services
- Business development meetings and/or pitches (if you're looking for coaching work in businesses or other organizations)
- Administration, including sending forms and exercises to clients, plus sending out letters, e-mails, brochures and bills/invoices
- Monitoring your accounts and working out how much tax you need to pay
- Taking calls from people who may never turn into clients
- Your own personal and professional development

And don't forget holidays, lunches and travel time.

OK, so once you've worked out how much income you're likely to have, you now need to factor in your *expenditure*. The amount of money you invest in launching and maintaining your coaching practice depends very much on you.

If you have an accountant or book-keeper, they can help you with some of the calculations.

Here are some of the expenses that you may have to think about:

- Marketing to launch your practice
- On-going marketing costs, e.g. networking, website hosting
- Stationery and postage
- Telephone calls and line rental
- Office equipment, e.g. desk, chair, filing cabinet, printer
- Coaching premises or hired meeting rooms
- Income tax
- Valued Added Tax (VAT)
- Bank charges – if you have a business account

Who pays for coaching?

Coaching is a fantastic tool for helping people from all walks of life to achieve more. Many coaches, perhaps you are one of them, want to make a positive difference in the world.

Unfortunately, not everyone can afford to pay for coaching, so if you are relying on your coaching practice to keep a roof over your head and food in your belly, it's best to concentrate your marketing first on those who are in a position to pay your fees.

Of course, once you have a steady flow of coaching work that is covering your expenses and allowing you to live life in the way that you want to, you may consider donating some of your time to pro-bono or unpaid work.

This is what I was talking about when I told you about Maslow's hierarchy of needs earlier on. Do things that help you achieve self-actualization when the other needs are being met.

The surveys give us a good indication of the types of people who are paying for coaching. According to the ICF survey:

- 46.9% of respondents said that they were coaching managers
- 45.9% said that they were coaching executives

These aren't mutually exclusive. The same coach who said, *"I'm coaching managers"* could also be ticking the box and saying *"I'm coaching executives as well."*

- 35.1% of the respondents were coaching entrepreneurs
- 30.1% were coaching business owners
- 28.1% were coaching professionals in private practice

What do we notice about this? Well, those who are prepared to invest in coaching are either individuals in the higher income brackets or organizations investing in the development of their senior staff or owners.

Summary

- Coaches risk charging too little or too much when they launch
- Maslow's hierarchy of needs shows us that to avoid inner conflict we should concentrate on the basic needs first
- Many coaches take part-time jobs to support themselves when they are starting out
- On average coaches spend 5-10 hours a week coaching
- Many coaches are now quoting their fees on a monthly basis rather than an hourly basis
- Coaching can be worth much more to the client than the amount of money they initially paid for it
- On average, coaches charge between £55 and £85 per hour
- The hourly charge increases when coaching is bought as part of a package as other services are bundled into the price
- When calculating how much to charge, take into account the hours you'll be spending on activities that don't earn you money, e.g. doing the administration
- The people who pay for coaching tend to be in the middle-upper income brackets and work as managers, executives, professionals or business owners

Section 2 Start Shooting Those Ducks!

Now that you're focused about the clients you want to work with and what you've got on offer, it's time to start telling the world that you're out there!

In this section, you'll discover:

- How to construct a marketing message that your clients will take notice of
- When to give up and when to persist
- How to tap into the networks you already have
- Which networking groups to go to
- How to strike up a conversation with a complete stranger
- Tactics for getting featured in the press
- The *real* secret about effective PR
- How to get booked as a pubic speaker
- Steps to developing your internet strategy
- Ways to get your website to do your selling for you
- Using advertising to spread your message quickly
- What responses you can expect from direct marketing
- The essentials that you need to have on your stationery
- Exactly what to say when prospective clients contact you
- How to 'sell yourself' to businesses and organizations
- When and how to put a marketing plan together
- Tips on delegating to other people

You'll also be able to read interviews with successful niche coaches about how they got started. Look out for the 'Coach Files' at the end of this book.

chapter five Your Marketing Message

FIVE Your Marketing Message

Right, you've decided on your niche, you know how you want to position yourself and set your prices, now it's time to start telling the world that you're out there!

Understand who you're aiming at

It's really key to get the message right, and targeted at the right people because it can be very, very frustrating going out and doing all of your marketing and then finding out that no one's interested because it's not relevant to them.

It's easy to do this with networking groups. If you're not clear about the kind of people that you want to be talking to, you can end up doing a lot of networking and giving up a lot of your evenings, your mornings, your lunchtimes – but find that you're actually talking to the wrong people, the people who aren't going to fit in with the kind of coaching that you do.

Have a benefits-driven message

Clients want to know what's in it for them. They want to know what the benefits of coaching are much more than they want to know how it works, or how many certificates you've got on your wall.

Think about the type of coaching you want to do – what's in it for your clients? What do they get from being coached by *you*?

Know your outcome

Also think about the desired outcome – what do you want to *happen* as a result of people being exposed to your marketing? What *exactly* do you want people to do when they hear or see your marketing message? What action do you want them to take? In order for your message to generate responses, you must tell people what to do to take things forward – don't trust that they'll telepathically know what to do.

If you want them to phone you, tell them to do that.

If you want them to fill in a box on your website to get a FREE Report, tell them.

If you want them to come to the front of your seminar and sign up for a FREE initial consultation, tell them.

A confused mind always says, 'No'

It's great to have options available for people, but having options means having to think about it and, for people with busy lives, they don't always have the time to think about things properly.

This issue is especially important when you're aiming to get responses from your marketing. Giving people the option of phoning you, emailing you, sending you a letter or filling in a form on your website may result in there being a much lower response than saying, *"Call this number now and leave your details to receive a FREE report on how you can get more time with your children."*

Carrot or stick approach?

Are you a *Towards* or an *Away-From* person? One of the lessons from NLP is that people tend to be one or the other and your prospective clients are the same.

They will set their goals to:

1. Move towards something, or
2. Move away from something

This is a concept that you can use in your marketing – are people having coaching to make something happen or to avoid something?

Once you start to understand your clients, you will know instinctively which of those two approaches is going to be better.

Some *towards* messages

"Discover how you can get more done in less time and take the rest of the day off! Book your tickets today for this sell-out seminar by calling..."

"My coach helped me to make 50% more sales than ever before – and she can do it for you! Phone now for a FREE consultation and to find out more."

"7 Simple steps to a calmer and friendlier you. Enter your e-mail address below to receive your FREE report instantly."

Some *away-from* messages

"My long hours cost me my marriage – don't let it happen to you."

"Are you fed up with your job, but don't know how to move on?"

"Dreading that Best Man speech? Here's how to make sure they're laughing with *you, not at you..."*

Increasing your success rate when talking about your marketing message

There are a number of different points that I'm going to go through now which will really increase your chances of success with the marketing that you do and also when you're talking to people one-on-one.

The actual timing when you're talking to them

It may be a good time for *you* to speak about coaching, but what about your client? If you've called somebody up in response to an e-mail or other request from them, just check that it's actually a good time for *them* to talk – this applies to both personal and business clients.

The reason is that if you're trying to get your message across and they've *literally* got to walk out the door in five minutes to go and pick the kids up, they're not going to be in the right frame of mind to listen to you and really take things in.

Consider that when you're calling on their mobile phone, they might be driving and on a hands-free speaker phone system (and their passenger might be listening), they could be up a ladder or have their hands full with their shopping. They could be in a meeting or in a public place or open-plan office where they can't talk openly.

When you're on the receiving end of a call it's *really nice* to have someone say, *"Is it a good time to talk?"*

And then you have the opportunity if it isn't a good time to talk to say something like, *"Oh, I'm really sorry. I need to get something done, but I can talk in about half an hour. Can we speak then?"*

Actually speaking to the right person

Something I learned in my years working in sales is that you can spend a lot of time promoting yourself to the wrong person.

Now you might think that this is just in the business context where you spend your whole time speaking to the PA, the gatekeeper or the manager and they're not actually the decision-maker.

You can also find this when you're promoting yourself to personal clients. For example, if you were targeting students, they might not actually have the money to pay for coaching. So you might be better off targeting your message to the parents who do have the money to pay for it and would be willing to invest in their child's success.

Another thing is, is your client actually in the market to be able to buy coaching at the moment? It might be something that they need to think about for a while. It might be something that they need to get a second opinion on from someone else, or ask the person who holds the purse strings.

Have you got an attitude problem?

Your attitude and your beliefs about yourself, your abilities, what you can do for your clients and whether they're going to say yes, always affects your success rate.

Do you ever, before you pick up the phone, say to yourself, *"I just know they're going to say no"*? STOP! Don't pick up the phone, because you're going to be right!

If you are confident, enthusiastic and clear about what you can do – your clients will pick up on that. Equally, if you have doubts, your clients will pick up on it too.

If you feel uncomfortable promoting yourself, then just talk about your success stories. What have your clients achieved? I'm sure that you can speak really enthusiastically about clients that you've worked with and the results they've had. Would you feel better about this than going out there and saying, *"Me, me, me – I'm brilliant!"*, which many people feel uncomfortable about.

How to win clients and influence referrers

Dr Robert Cialdini found that there are three main factors to building a relationship.

1. Similarity

People like people like them. What have you got in common with your clients? How can you show that you have empathy and rapport with them?

2. Praise

People like to know what you like about them. So when you're meeting prospective clients – what is it that you like about them? How could you tell them that you like something about them?

And it doesn't have to be really *creepy*. It doesn't have to come across that you're sucking up to them. You could say to a client, *"Thanks for calling on time. What I really like about you is that you're punctual."* Or make a point of saying that someone has called you back when they said they would. Or that they have made time to see you, or that they're really enthusiastic and bubbly that morning.

You can also say things like, *"I really like talking to people like you!"*

In your marketing materials, you can state the kinds of people that you really enjoy working with. Because if they're that kind of person, they'll read it and say to themself, *"Oh good! They really enjoy working with people like me."*

3. Cooperation

People like to achieve *their* goals – not yours. So find out what is important to your clients, rather than what is important to you and use that to develop a good marketing message.

Use your client's language ... word for word

As coaches, we're always taught to paraphrase and to use some of the language that our clients are using. This helps the client to know that they've been heard and understood.

There is research to back this up. In a study reported in Dr Cialdini's *Influence at Work* online magazine, waiters and waitresses who repeated orders back to customers, using the exact same words that the customers had used, received bigger tips.

Customers felt more valued when their order was repeated rather than when the waiter/waitress said, *"Uh-huh"*, *"Yes"* or *"OK"*.

I think this is really relevant when you're first having conversations with prospective clients. So, if they say to you, *"I'm feeling under pressure at work,"* you say, *"When you're feeling under pressure at work, what is it that makes you feel this way? How would you like things to be different?"*

The power of persistence and the reality of repetition

How many times should you talk to or communicate with someone before giving up? Until they flatly say, *"No"*? Even then they might mean, *"Not right now"*!

It's estimated that a person needs to be exposed to communications from a new supplier/contact seven times before they will trust them enough to buy from them. These statistics are for product marketing and I'd suggest that it's a minimum of seven exposures for services marketing. So, since you're marketing services, you need to be prepared to have some sort of contact with prospective clients seven or more times before they will become a client. 'Contact' can mean talking to them, e-mailing them, meeting them, them reading an article or a newsletter, them hearing you on the radio, and so on. Many coaches run one or two adverts, send out a sales letter, make a few phone calls and wonder why they aren't drowning in new clients. The reality is that you need to be constantly marketing yourself.

With all of the information competing for your attention every single day, you have to filter things out and sometimes you miss important information because your internal 'spam filter' is set too high.

Just take a moment now and think about what some of your friends do for a living. Even with the friends and family that we see very often, it's quite difficult to remember precisely what people do, even if they've told you a few times.

These are people who are supposed to be our friends! It's even harder to remember what acquaintances are doing! It's vital that you keep reinforcing your message. But make sure that the message is clear – *a confused mind always says, "No".*

Another reason that it can take a while for people to really absorb your message and trust that you're the right coach for them is that they're watching and waiting to see whether you're having success with other people. This is when telling success stories and using testimonials can be very powerful – it can speed up the amount of time it takes for people to trust that you'll do a good job.

> Soon after I started my own coach training, I worked with someone for just one session. At the end of it, he said, *"I've realized that I don't want to be coached, I want someone to tell me what to do."* We shook hands and kept the lines of communication open. A year later, I had a call out of the blue, *"Hannah, I keep seeing your articles everywhere and I get your monthly newsletter. I've decided that I'd like to try coaching again and I'd like you to be my coach."*

Keep in regular contact with people

The beauty of having a regular newsletter and getting articles published is that it gives you a reason to get back in touch with people and keep reminding them that you're there – with no pressure. It keeps you in the forefront of their minds so that when they're ready they know where you are and they can get in touch.

But there will be some people who enquire about coaching and then change their minds. These are the people who, when you're talking to them on the phone, will say, *"I just need to have a think about it."*

What do you think? *"Oh no! What if they go away to think about it – and never come back?"*

Something that I've said to clients that has worked quite well is to say to them, *"OK, that's absolutely fine if you want to have a think about it. In my experience, I've found when clients say they want to think about it, it means that they are still unclear about something or there is some other issue. Is that the case with you?"*

And that's usually the time that they'll say, *"Actually I just had a big gas bill and I can't afford it right now, but maybe next month I can."* Or there's something else that they're just not sure about.

It then gives you that opportunity to have the discussion with them to find out what the situation is, to reassure them that they're not going to be pushed into it and that they can come back when the time is right.

This is good because otherwise they can be too embarrassed to call you again. They might think that you'll be really angry with them if they don't want to have a session right now and don't want the confrontation. It's easier to sneak away and never speak to you again and then when the time is right, go off and get coached by somebody else – after you've done all that hard work warming them up – because they feel too embarrassed to come back. Keep the lines of communication open and make it OK for people to come back to you when they're ready. It doesn't hurt to send them a personal e-mail a month after you've first spoken to them and then a gentle nudge every three months to say hi and ask how they're getting along.

Summary

- Understand who you're aiming at and what's in it for them – clients want to know what *they* are going to get from hiring you as their coach
- Keep your message simple and tell clients what you want them to do next
- Think about whether you want to use a *towards* message or an *away-from* message
- When you're phoning people about coaching, always check whether they are able to talk and if it's convenient to talk now
- Be aware of your attitudes and beliefs as they can influence the way that your message comes across
- Dr Cialdini found that there are three ways to build relationships – similarity, praise, cooperation
- Use your client's exact words when speaking to them
- Clients may need to be exposed to your marketing message seven times before feeling comfortable about taking the next step with you
- Keep the lines of communication open and make it easy for clients to come back to you when they are ready

chapter six **Networking**

SIX Networking

There's an old saying: *"It's not* ***what*** *you know, but* ***who*** *you know."* Well, these days it's not enough to **know** the right people. They must know you and rate you as one of the 'good guys'. So the modern slant is: *"It's not what you know, but who knows you."*

"But I'm just starting out in coaching, people don't know me."

This is where networking comes into its own. Coaching is about honest communication between two people, isn't it? And so is networking.

What is networking about?

Say, *"You've got to network"* to most people starting out in coaching and they panic. The common misconception is that you'll have to plonk yourself into a room of strangers and start selling yourself. Anyone who's ever been filled with dread at turning up to a party and not knowing anyone will understand how this feels. But you needn't feel like that.

True networking is *not* about selling yourself, it's discovering how you can help the other person you're talking to, to connect with suitable contacts. That's right, helping the other person to connect with someone you know.

"But I don't know anyone!"

It's said that the average person knows around 250 people. It's not just limited to your immediate friends and family, but people you come into contact with while going about your daily life – your doctor, solicitor, accountant, hairdresser, people from your church, gym or football club, the list goes on.

EXERCISE

Go through the names and numbers you've got saved in your mobile/cell phone or the people in your e-mail address book and count how many more people you know. Then think about people you used to work with, people you went to college with, the list goes on! Now, do you think that some of those people might be willing to help you to get some new clients?

Established referral routes

Unlike other 'helping professions' there is no established referral system for coaching. What I mean by this is that if someone were feeling down and thought that they might need a counsellor, they would probably make an appointment with their GP who would refer them on to someone.

That said, there are some forward-thinking doctors who are recommending that their clients talk to a life coach rather than a therapist or counsellor when they do not require a therapeutic solution, for example if they are unhappy at work. This is really refreshing and means that there are opportunities for coaches working around stress and work/life balance to speak to local GPs and explain more about what they do and how they work.

Equally for business and executive coaches, there is no formal referral process, but they are starting to develop through management consultants, business groups and associations, and training companies, as well as through professional bodies such as the CIPD (Chartered Institute of Personnel and Development).

In the absence of established referral routes, it's up to each and every one of us to network and build relationships with people who are already moving in the same circles as our target clients and who can make recommendations and referrals to build our client base.

ANOTHER EXERCISE

From the list you put together in the last exercise, identify three people who might be able to give you the best contacts. They should also be people who you would be comfortable just picking up the phone and talking to. Arrange to meet them for coffee and a chat during the next week. When you call, tell them that you're now working as a professional coach and you'd appreciate any help or advice they could give you in growing your practice. Ask them about your marketing message and whether it would appeal to people they know. Ask who they know who might need your help. Finally, ask them if there's anything you can do to help them – after all, you've now got loads of contacts!

Note: Remember to take your business cards with you!

Tip #1: Arrange one of your meetings with your accountant – they will have loads of contacts, loads of experience of dealing with new businesses and they want you to be successful!

Tip #2: Use your rapport building skills to enhance the meeting.

Asking for help

You may not believe it, but people really do want to help. What they get from it is feeling that they're knowledgeable about their subject and that they have good contacts, as well as the feel-good factor of helping a fellow human being.

There are very, very few people that I've met in the time that I've been running my business, that don't actually want to help. And to be honest, they're the ones that don't last in business very long.

The people who know about building up a practice or a business know that you need to talk to one another and you need to help each other out, because what goes around, comes around. It's business karma.

BNI (Business Network International) is one of the largest referral networks with local groups in most areas. Their philosophy is 'givers gain'. It's not just a gimmicky strapline – it is true. The more that you give to other people, the more it comes back to you – and not always from the same person that you gave the help to.

Why network at all?

Why shouldn't we just rely on:

- Press releases?
- Advertising?
- Our website?
- Sending out letters?

Well, the first main reason is that if you're networking, you're actually meeting people.

When you decide to work with a coach you have to feel that the chemistry is right and meeting a coach for the first time at a networking event is almost like interviewing them, to a certain extent.

And that's one of the reasons you really need to look and feel the part. Because when you're out networking – and even when you're talking to your normal contacts – people will make judgments based on their first impressions and that could make the difference between them recommending you – and not.

Personal recommendations or word of mouth marketing, as networking is sometimes called, is *really, really powerful.*

People buy people

Have you noticed in the TV informercials they always have someone saying something along the lines of, *"Yes, I used the Super Thigh Machine and it was fantastic!"*? It's because when you hear what an actual person says about a product, it's more credible. People buy people.

Networking is a great way to pick up some good contacts and to get personal recommendations so that real people spread the word like the informercials. Also, it's a brilliant way to get useful contacts for *you*. When you're starting out, you need to think about who is going to design your logo, your website – and it's much better to go to someone who has been recommended to you, or who you have met at a networking event, than just going through the Yellow Pages and making decisions blind.

You could find your accountant, solicitor – even people to rent office space from or space to do your coaching in through your networks. But the main reason that people start networking is to find people who they can refer business to and who will refer business back to them.

Another reason to network is that it's a great way to get talking to other business owners in a more sociable setting. Sharing experiences about what it's like to set up a business, what the challenges are that you come across, what the pitfalls are and the lessons that people have learned along the way.

'Fake it till you make it'

Have you heard that expression? The idea is that you make out that you're already really, really successful and people will come to you. Yes, I believe in that up to a point – an air of success and experience puts your prospective clients' and referrers' minds at ease – they're confident you can do a good job. The danger is that it can stop you asking for help because you're afraid people will see through you but if you do say to people, *"Well, I've been doing this for a few months now. I'm really looking for a contact in _______, do you know anyone?"* They can help you out or they can find you someone who can help you.

Types of networking events

There are many ways to network and some are more formal than others. Some require you to take out a membership and with some you need to make a commitment to be involved with the group for a minimum period of time.

Formal networking groups

These are the groups that are set up for the sole purpose of members referring business contacts to one another and these include organizations such as BNI and BRE (Business Referral Exchange). Formal groups have regular meetings, usually weekly. It's very structured and everybody knows why they're there. There's no pretence that you're there to make the best of friends for life (though that does happen too) – you're there to get some good business contacts and start to get some work yourself, and bring other people work. These groups tend to be popular with coaches targeting business clients.

Online networking

Recently, online networking has become popular, with one of the largest online business networks at Ecademy (www.ecademy.com). Online networks allow you to upload your own profile, view other people's profiles and advertise your services to people as well as building networks of contacts. Ecademy also organizes live networking events, where you can meet people in person. You can find online networking groups which are relevant for your niche by ... searching online!

Seminar/event networking

When you attend seminars and other events, remember to take your business cards because there will usually be opportunities for you to meet other people and network. You can find out about local seminars and events by contacting your Chamber of Commerce, other business organizations or specialist groups (e.g. Women in Business). They usually have events that you can attend every month without having to be a member.

The key is to pick events that your target clients are likely to attend. For example, if you notice a seminar about time management and you coach busy professionals on work/life balance you may be able to meet prospective clients there. Of course, there is the danger that the people who need help most are too busy to make time for a seminar about how to manage their time!

Whenever there is a speaker at an event, you can use this as a conversation starter; for example, *"Have you seen Fred Bloggs speak before?"* or *"What interested you in this topic?"* Remember to talk to the speaker after they have been on and congratulate them on their presentation – networking with the speaker can be very productive.

> **Sneaky tip:** One of my previous bosses used the Q and A session at the end of events to promote his business. He did this by standing up so everyone could see him and then saying his name and company name before asking his question.
>
> **Warning:** Don't use the Q and A session to embarrass the speaker by asking awkward questions or picking holes in their presentation. Even if their presentation stinks, they won't thank you for pointing it out and the audience will think you're a know-it-all – not good for business.

Niche networking

The absolute best way to network is to find out where and how all the people in your niche meet to talk about issues and challenges that you can help with. Here are some examples:

Targeting HR professionals?

Check out your local CIPD branch.

Targeting other professionals?

Look up the website for their trade body or association to find out where and when they meet. Check their trade press or other publications to find out when conferences are happening.

Targeting individuals?

Where do people who would be interested in your services get together? Depending on your niche, you could consider mind, body and spirit exhibitions, careers fairs, gyms, investment seminars or any other specialist events.

Networking with people you already know

If you already have contacts, use them! It's much easier to ask people who know you for help. Who do you know in the list below?

- Friends and family
- Colleagues
- Current/previous employer (s)
- Current/past clients
- Other coaches

When you next see your friends and family, make a mental note to ask how things are at work or with their business, as well as talking about social subjects. It's amazing how many opportunities are right there in front of you when you ask the right questions. Use your coaching and rapport building skills to find out more about who they know and if they'd be willing to introduce you to them.

For example, if you think that complementary therapists might be treating your prospective clients, the next time someone mentions having a massage or a treatment, ask who they went to and if they could introduce you to them. Equally, if you think that accountants might be able to refer clients to you, when someone mentions their tax return, ask if they have an accountant and if they could introduce you. Use active listening skills to uncover opportunities.

Many coaches find their first clients through people they work with or through the companies that they've worked for. Could this be the case for you too? It's a sad fact that in their hurry to start a new life and a new career some coaches let work connections and contacts fizzle away to nothing. Some even burn their bridges completely by being a bit too frank in their exit interview. Giving your boss a one-fingered salute and screaming, *"I never liked any of you anyway!"* at everyone when you leave the office for the last time may not be the best move

You already know and understand the people you work with and you have experienced their challenges first hand, so when you do make a break for it and set up on your own, your old work colleagues could be your best clients.

Remember: *Take your address/contacts book with you when you leave. You never know when you might want to call someone you've dealt with in the past.*

Your current and past coaching clients are a good source of referral business because they know what it's like to be coached by you and can sing your praises. When you finish working with a client, it's OK to say, *"I'd really like more clients like you"* and ask them how you would go about attracting more people like them. They may even give you names and numbers of people to contact.

Finally, there is value in networking with other coaches in your area because you might be able to refer business between you. They may not want to coach the kind of people that you do want to coach or on the topics you want to coach on, and vice versa. That's where it becomes really important to understand who it is you work with so that you can be clear about the boundaries and when someone should refer a client to you. This applies both with business/corporate clients and personal clients. You could have a loose reciprocal arrangement or a more formal associate arrangement, where the coach referring the work keeps some of the fees the client pays – in the same way that an agency would take a commission.

WAIT! Before you get stuck in...

It's time to do a bit of self-coaching and ask yourself a few questions:

- What do you want to achieve through networking?
- Who do you want to meet?
- Where could you meet them?
- Who could connect you with them?
- What do you want to happen?
- What are you going to do about it?
- What will you say when you do meet that person?

You can spend every breakfast, lunchtime and evening going to lots of networking events, but if you're not quite sure why you're there you're wasting your time. And let's face it, if you're charging by the hour, time literally is money. Focus your attention on the networks that generate *results*. In the same way that you want to get a return on your investment from any other form of marketing, it's important to keep a record of all the business you've got through your different networks. Before you even set foot in one of these networking events, who are the kinds of contacts that you want to meet? Who is your ideal client?

If your fairy godmother appeared and said, *"I know absolutely everybody on the planet. Who can I introduce you to?"*, what would you say? Be ready with an answer, because it's much easier for people to help you if you tell them as specifically as possible who it is that you want to meet. If you want to coach a celebrity – tell everyone that you want to coach that celebrity! Because hey! somebody might know them.

That celebrity could be your gold standard client. If you wanted to coach Brad Pitt, who do you know that might know people who know people who can introduce you? Remember, you might only get one shot at impressing people who can connect you with public figures. Make sure that you can live up to the claims you make about yourself.

Give people some triggers to listen out for. So if you want to coach people on work/life balance, say to the people that you meet, *"If you ever hear someone saying 'I'm working really long hours and I don't get time with my family', that's the time to mention me. That's the time to tell them what I do."* Tell them what to listen out for and tell them how they can help you.

What goes around, comes around, so always ask people how you can help them and who you can introduce them to. A handy tip is to write what they're looking for on the back of their business card, but do be aware of how different cultures treat business cards because in some parts of Asia you could cause offence by defacing someone's card.

Hunting versus farming

Hunters are the people who will slap a few business cards in your hand, not really listen to what you do, and just want to talk about themselves, and try to sell something to you there and then. They don't last long in networking because what will happen is they will exhaust the group. They will get as much business as they can from the people that are there and they'll move on. And you won't see them again – thank goodness!

Farmers, in networking, are the ones that build the relationships. They plant the seeds, they water them, they *nurture* those little seedlings because one day they will bear fruit. And you're never quite sure which of those little seedlings will bear fruit for you.

When you're at networking events, you're not there to sell to the person in front of you. If they're interested in what you're promoting – great! That's a bonus. But what you're there for is to:

- Build contacts
- Make connections
- Build relationships with people

And build that relationship to such an extent that they recommend you to lots and lots of people.

You've probably heard some networkers say, *"It's a numbers game. The more people you speak to, the more chance you've got of getting the right sort of contact."*

That's true to a point. But if you spend the whole of a networking meeting flitting from one person to the next, you're not going to remember what all of them do. And they're certainly not going to remember what *you* do. Spend your time building up some good quality contacts and nurturing them, by following-up.

How do you approach people at business networking events?

What happens if you walk in there, slightly late and everybody seems to be engrossed in conversation and it's just like walking into a party where you don't know anyone – what do you do?

Start by looking for people who are on their own – especially people who look a bit lost – if they've got a drink in their hand, they'll probably be sipping quite regularly to cover up the fact that they're uncomfortable. If there are no people on their own, find the host of the event – they can usually be found at the signing-in table. Say to them something along the lines of:

"Hello, I'm ______, it's the first time I've been here. I'm a coach specializing in ______ and the kind of people I really want to meet today (or tonight) are ______. Would you be kind enough to introduce me to a few people?"

And if they're a good host, they'll do it. If not, or if there's nobody around that can help you with that – look for the buffet table, look for people admiring the artwork or people looking out into the gardens, so that there's something neutral and mutual that you can strike up a conversation on.

You can start it off with, *"Have you been to one of these things before?"* Yes, I know it sounds a little bit corny and it's like the old chat up line, *"Do you come here often?"* But it is a good opener. Talk about anything that you can think of (within reason!) and ask questions.

People love to talk about themselves, so ask questions about what they do, what they enjoy and if they're in business, ask about how they got started and how their business has evolved.

If there's a speaker at the event, go and talk to them. If you have spoken at events, you'll know that sometimes you put your heart and soul into giving a good presentation and then *no one* comes and speaks to you afterwards!

As a speaker, it can be very embarrassing when everyone rushes off to the bar and you're left packing up on your own. When someone does come over and is interested in what you have to say, it's great. Just in case you're thinking that the speaker doesn't want to be bothered by audience members, consider why the speaker is there.

Like you, the speaker is there for self-promotion and to promote their business. Often the speaker is not paid to speak at groups and networking events. They do it to showcase their services and get people interested in:

- What they do
- Signing up for a newsletter
- Attending another (paid) workshop or seminar
- Buying their services

They may even be looking for one-to-one coaching or consulting work from it. The speaker is there to try and get business so when they just get left alone by all the people who are listening to them, it's really disappointing for them. How would you like to be treated if you were in their position? Getting to know the people who speak in your area can open up doors for you and once you have a good relationship with them, there may be opportunities to tap into their networks or even do some joint promotion. Speakers are often asked by event organizers who they know who speaks on a particular topic – they might just recommend you!

The four deadly sins of networking

Sin #1 – Excluding people from conversations

Most people at networking events don't know each other and it takes courage for individuals to approach a group. If someone tries to involve themselves in a group discussion, welcome them in and listen to what they have to say.

Sin #2 – Hard selling

You are not there to make a 'sale', but to build contacts and relationships. If someone shows an interest in your services, by all means talk to them about what you can do, but don't ram it down their throat by telling them that if they don't use you, their life will come crashing down around them.

Sin #3 – Monopolizing people

Everyone's there to network, that means talking to several people – not just you. Even if you're getting on really well with someone and you could quite happily spend the rest of the time with them, don't. Instead, say something like, *"Well I suppose we'd better start mingling, hadn't we? I've love to find out more about what you do – shall I give you a call tomorrow/next week? Here's my card, do you have one?"*

Sin #4 – Looking over people's shoulders while they're talking

It's rude and yes, people *can* see when you're doing it. You might be glancing at the buffet coming in or you've just spotted someone you know, but the person on the receiving end will feel unimportant. Keep good eye contact and make the time you spend with them meaningful.

The elevator pitch

An elevator pitch is a method of getting your message across in 20–30 seconds in a way that will interest your prospective client and give you an opportunity to swap business cards. It's called an elevator pitch because you'd typically have only 20–30 seconds alone in an elevator with someone before one of you has to get out!

Your elevator pitch should have a benefits-driven message that tells people what they'd get from working with you. It can also include information about the kinds of clients you like working with and what people should do if they think that someone they know might be a potential client for you: what should they say to them?

EXERCISE

Your elevator pitch could be used in a number of different settings listed below. Fill in all the ways you can think of to use your elevator pitch:

- When meeting someone new at a networking event
- Introducing yourself as a speaker at a seminar
- On your voicemail messages
- When cold-calling

The elevator pitch is best used for when you have very limited time, when you're talking to a group (e.g. at a breakfast networking group) or when you're in speed networking events. These are the ones where you sit opposite someone for a couple of minutes each. You each get to talk about what you do, and then you move on to the next person.

When you start talking to people about your coaching practice, you can use elements from your elevator pitch. But it can sound a little bit unnatural if you are in that one-to-one situation. So what do you do?

Well, like any good coach, ask the person you're talking to lots of questions because people love the sound of their own voice.

In getting them to talk first, you get them to open up and tell you about the areas where they're doing well, and the areas where they're not doing so well. In those areas where they're not doing so well, there may be opportunity for you to talk about what you do and how you can help.

Don't make the mistake of trying to coach someone at a networking event. They may not want you to and may take your challenging questions as an intrusion. Personally, I don't like it when coach friends of mine try to stealth-coach me, i.e. without my consent. In normal conversations people want to have real discussions, have differences of opinions and get to know the person they're talking to.

Just because your emphasis is on the client when you're in a session, it doesn't mean that you have to blend into the background *outside* of your sessions. You are still a person with something to say. You have opinions. You have your own life experiences. You are interesting to listen to. You can have a difference of opinion with someone and still be non-judgmental. You can be a coach and be yourself.

Recently I went to hear BJ Cunningham speak. He's a branding specialist and something he said stuck in my mind (I'm paraphrasing):

"If everyone likes you that means you're boring. If you've got something interesting to say, people will agree or disagree, but you can't please everyone."

Tell stories

In the days before writing, knowledge and experience was passed down through storytelling. Many of the key lessons in religious texts are made through storytelling, parable and metaphor. Children remember lessons when they are told them in story form. It's the way that humans learn easily.

You can use this to help people to remember what you're good at. You do this by telling them real success stories about clients you've worked with, without naming names. It helps you to achieve several outcomes:

- It shows that you already have clients and you have experience
- People want to know what they'd get from coaching and stories illustrate this well
- You're not talking about 'me, me, me' all the time, clients come first

If you can give people some examples of what you've done for other clients that then gives *them* something that they can talk to other people about. They can say:

"Oh! I met this person at a networking event the other night and she was telling me about a client who she'd worked with who was in just your situation. In just a few sessions, they'd resolved it and moved on. I think I've got one of her cards here – there you go. Why don't you give her a call?"

When should you exchange business cards with people?

The obvious answer is when they ask for yours or give you one of theirs. You can speed up the process by asking them for their card. Say, *"That's really interesting! I know someone who might be interested in what you do. Do you have your card on you?"* then take one of their cards and that gives you an opportunity to say, *"Since we're exchanging cards anyway – here's one of mine."*

Don't give them a great big bundle of cards because it's a bit presumptuous that they're going to go off and do all your networking for you! If they want extra cards, they'll ask you for them.

Think about how you would react if someone you'd just met said:

"Here you go – here are ten of my cards. Take them and give them out to all your friends and send them out to all your business contacts and associates."

Hmm ... would you do it? Or would you keep one and throw out the rest?

What if you get stuck with someone?

There will be times when someone tries to monopolize *you* at an event. The best strategy is to just be open about it, but I don't mean you should say, *"I'm stuck with you and I want to escape."* Say something along the lines of, *"We're here to network, aren't we? It's been interesting finding out about your business and I'd like to keep in touch, but I'm sure that you'd like time to network with other people too. Let's move over to the bar/table/other group and see who else is here."*

You've both come with the same agenda – that is to talk to lots of people. And they're not achieving their goal by spending the whole evening with you. No matter how comfortable it gets for them, you're not actually doing them any favours by staying with them for the whole event.

But if you really are stuck with someone and you can't see any prospect of the two of you working together in any shape or form, then start to break rapport with them. You could even consider committing one of the deadly sins of networking (see earlier). If you really do get stuck, you can always go to the toilet and jump out the window! Checking that you're not on the fifth floor before you do so!

Seriously though, you can do things like walk over to the bar together and try to introduce them to someone else either on the way or when you're there.

Following up with people

This is where a lot of people fall down on networking. You go to all these events, you come back with a stack of business cards and then nothing happens.

Don't rely on the other person taking the initiative. As a rule of thumb, the day after you've been to a networking event, it's good to drop everybody you met an e-mail – but don't do it as a blanket e-mail for everyone. Do an individual e-mail to each of the people you've met.

Put something personal in there to say something like, *"It was really interesting to hear about your business"* – or whatever you were talking about. *"I'm going to put my thinking cap on and see if I can come up with any contacts for you."*

Then if you can come up with some contacts, drop them an e-mail a couple of days later and say, *"You know we were talking about how you really wanted to talk to accountants? I've come up with one or two people who I think I can introduce you to – is it OK to give them your details?"* Or, you can give them the details of the person who wants to speak to them – so start introducing people to one another.

If you think it's appropriate, follow it up with a phone call to say, *"I've been thinking a bit more about what you were telling me when we met. I just wondered if this kind of person will be useful for you?"*

Even if you're really not sure if it's the kind of person they want to talk to, the fact that you've picked up the phone and you're still thinking about them a few days later will really stand out – because not many people do this.

Now, the reason for following up with people is this: you know it's going to take about seven communications before somebody trusts you enough to start to recommend you to other people, or take you on as their coach themselves.

Doing this follow-up is going to make you stand out because you've gone to the trouble to get to know them, to understand what you can do for them – before you've even asked them to do anything for you.

Offer to help them in some way, if there is anything that you can do to help – if you hear about another networking event that you think they might be interested in, drop them a note and say:

"I saw this and thought it might be your kind of thing. I'm thinking about going. Do you fancy just popping in and saying 'hi' first – and then we can go in and network?" But don't fall into the trap of them thinking you're inviting them there to talk to *them* for the whole event. Make the point that you are there to network and say, *"Maybe we can maximize our opportunities for networking if we start off together and we can introduce each other to people we know."*

When you first start networking, it can be useful to keep in touch with most of the people you meet because there's a chance that they might be able to connect you with clients. As you start to narrow your focus, you should spend more time cultivating the relationships that are likely to result in business.

Make sure that all the people that you know, know what you're looking for. That also applies to when you're meeting people socially – when you're talking to friends, when you're talking to family – and they ask how it's going. Tell them! Don't just say, *"Oh yes, it's getting better. It's picking up."*

Say things like, *"It's going well, but you know what? The person that I really want to talk to is (whoever it is) – don't suppose you know anyone who knows them, do you?"* Or say, *"I've been really trying to get into this group of people, do you know anyone that might be able to get me an open door so that I can go in and talk to people?"*

At my BNI chapter, I started saying to the other people, *"I'm not asking you to recommend me to anyone. I'm looking to do some research at the moment. These are the kinds of people I want to talk to, to do my research."* They gave me loads of contacts who helped me with my research and then were interested in finding out more about coaching!

It's also a great way of arranging to meet people for coffee to:

- Find out about what their challenges are
- What kind of support they would be looking for
- Whether people like them would like one-to-one coaching, group coaching, workshops, tele-classes
- Find out what would actually be useful to them
- Find out how much they would be prepared to pay

Use your networks to help you with your market research in the pre-launch and launch phases of your practice.

Asking for referrals on more sensitive issues

If you are coaching people on sensitive issues, it might not be the best strategy to ask directly for referrals to clients, for example to people who have particular diseases or conditions or are facing certain situations. But that doesn't mean you can't network. Use your contacts to put you in touch with support groups, refuges, hospitals and charities, who can then refer people to you once you've built up a trusting relationship with them.

Remember the context

When people are attending business networking groups, they are in a business frame of mind. When they are attending mind, body and spirit exhibitions, they are in another frame of mind. Take care to attend the events where your target clients will have the right mindset.

The same person who wears a suit and attends high-profile functions may also do Tai Chi and be interested in spiritual healing in their own time. But if you try talking to them about spiritual coaching at a business function, your message might be lost on them as it's out of context. Equally, if you ran a seminar about improving the profitability of big business at a mind, body and spirit exhibition, your message might fall on deaf ears and, worse still you might damage your brand and create hostility towards you.

Networking nightmares

You can't please all the people all the time, and sometimes when you set out with the best intentions, you can fail to meet your objectives for your networking. That's OK, as long as you learn from it and have action plans for next time

When there's a speaker booked at an event, it's possible to turn up, listen to them and leave without networking with anyone! So what could you do if you turned up late to find everyone in their seats and the speaker has already started?

The first thing you can do is loiter in your seat and speak to the person next to you when the speaker finishes. If there's a buffet or bar afterwards, hang around and strike up conversations with people. Another option is to go and talk to the speaker or the organizers.

Who knows – the organizers might have an opportunity for someone to speak at the next event and that someone might as well be you! Grab the opportunity by both hands and build up relationships with people who can put you in front of eager audiences.

How many contacts is a good result from an event?

Difficult to say, but it's the quality, not the quantity that counts. You could walk away with twenty business cards, but not remember who any of them were by the following morning or you could meet two really good contacts who want to meet you and find out more about what you do.

It depends on your goals for networking. Are you going because you want to build a mailing list or because you want to tap into people's networks? If you're there to network, then focus on quality, not quantity, and quality contacts are made when you take time to get to know the person. It's not enough just to pick up lots of business cards and put them on a newsletter list – if they don't know who on earth you are. It's much better to spend time with fewer people initially. Concentrate on building relationships with them and asking them to introduce you to other people that they know – rather than trying to work a room.

Be generous and think about what they want to get from the relationship too. Who can you introduce them to? What goes around comes around and you're creating good karma. Even if you can't think of anyone to introduce them to, look for articles online that you think might be interesting to them. When you do find articles, send them over to them. I get a lot of things on newsletters and e-mail lists and I'll think that so-and-so would find this *really* interesting! And then I just forward it to them saying, *"I saw this and thought of you."* You don't really need any more than that. If you see something in the paper, photocopy it, cut it out and send it to the person who you think might be interested in it.

Even if it turns out to be completely irrelevant or they've already seen it, they will think, *"That's nice. They were thinking of me."*

What should I put on my business cards?

You business card is an essential piece of kit. You should always include all the contact details that you're comfortable giving out. For example, you may not feel comfortable giving out your home address on your business card. You could use a virtual office or a PO Box for postal correspondence or if you do face-to-face coaching from rented rooms or offices, you could include that address.

Include:

- Company name (if applicable)
- Your name
- Your title – this could be coach, life coach, business coach, director, owner, whatever you choose. I've even seen people with titles such as 'Head Honcho' or 'Dogsbody'. Just be careful to choose a title that your target clients will find acceptable – you want to appear as a professional, after all!
- Your address
- Your contact phone number
- Your e-mail address
- Your website (if you have one)

Don't forget that business cards have a front *and* a back! More and more people are using the back of their business card to convey their marketing message or to promote their newsletter/free introductory session offers. Try to leave a small amount of blank space on the front or back of the card to allow people whom you meet at networking events to write reminders to themselves about you.

When you're designing your business card, think about what your *clients* will think of it – not whether you like the colour or it's your favourite font.

What does your brand stand for? How do you want your clients to perceive you?

- If you want to look *cheap*, then by all means print a flimsy card cheaply from your colour printer at home. If you want to look like you're *worth your fees*, professional and experienced, you can do this by getting your cards printed properly onto good quality card.
- If you want to look *organized*, make sure that all your contact details are accurate and you get your new cards printed *before* you switch to your new phone number, e-mail address or postal address so that you won't ever be 'waiting for the cards to arrive from the printers'. If you want to look *disorganized*, then cross out your old details and put your new ones in.

- If you want to look *confused,* use lots of different colours, designs and fonts on one card. If you want to appear *focused* and *in control,* have your details presented very clearly using simple but effective designs. Less is more.

More and more people are buying electronic card readers to input people's details into their database or online address book. These card readers scan the business card and translate it into text. They find it easiest to read black on white and clear fonts when all the contact information is on one side of the card.

Getting referrals from your clients

You will remember from Chapter 4 on pricing that the ICF conducted a survey of coaches. One of the most shocking statistics in the survey was that only 31.8% of the coaches who were surveyed used any form of client satisfaction surveys.

Now I don't know about you but I think that that is *CRAZY*! Nearly 70% of coaches – seven out of ten coaches – are not getting feedback from their clients.

I think that's outrageous because how do you know if you're doing a good job unless you ask your clients?

If you ask for feedback in the context of a coaching session, and just say:

- What do you think?
- How am I doing?
- How would you rate me?

What are they going to tell you? *"I think you're great!" or "I think coaching's fantastic!"* Yes, your ego will get some massaging but it's not information that helps you to constantly improve.

You can get a different response when somebody is filling in a survey and sending it back to you. You're going to get a much more honest answer because people are going to tell you what you want to hear when you're face to face with them or on the phone.

Very few clients will confront you and say, *"I think you're rubbish!"* or *"I think you could have worked better on this particular area."*

As a coach you need to always get feedback from your clients. *Always, always, always* – because there will generally be something that you can improve on next time.

Also, *they're missing a trick here*! What better way to get a reference and a testimonial from your clients than when they're filling in your feedback form?

Generally what I do with a survey is start it off with a scale of one to five and say *"How did you rate your coach?"* Not how did you rate *me*, but how did you rate your coach so it seems a little bit more independent.

Give your clients an indication of how to interpret the scale, for example one could be 'Excellent' and five could be 'Poor'. Always have your middle mark as average or neutral. Because if you say, 'Great', 'Even better', 'Absolutely fantastic' – you're not really giving them any room to say, *"Actually, you could have done better."*

Ask people in your client satisfaction survey what things were like before the coaching. Then ask them what their goals were and how things have changed since they've been working with you. That helps you to build up something that you can use in a case study, if they give their permission for you to use it.

Ask them whether they'd be willing to give you comments that you can use in your promotional materials. Now you might think, *"Is that being a bit pushy? Will people say that they'll give their permission for it? What if they say no?"*

Well, I can tell you of all the clients I've ever worked with, I have never had a client who said, *"No I don't want you to use my comments."* And I give my clients the choice on whether their name appears in full with their job title or their company, or whether it is their initials and their occupation. So far, only one of my clients has *ever* said that they want to remain anonymous. They've all gone for full name, job title and company.

Don't be one of the almost 70% of coaches that doesn't ask for feedback from clients. You are missing out if you're not getting feedback. Doing it in a survey that you can e-mail to them and get them to either e-mail back or post back is *such an easy way* of doing it. If you just ask somebody to give you a testimonial – a lot of people won't know what a testimonial means, but they won't tell you that – or they'll put it off and put it off because they just don't know how to write one effectively.

So, if you use a feedback form, you can get them to answer questions that help them to write their own testimonial, without having to sit down and draft a long letter.

Finally, the feedback form is a great opportunity for you ask for referrals if you're too shy to ask your clients directly. You can say something like:

"Most of my clients come to me through word-of-mouth recommendations. Who do you know who might benefit from coaching? I am offering a free half-hour initial consultation where they can find out more about how coaching works. If you know someone who would benefit from this, please enter their details below and I will send them some information."

Your current and past clients know what coaching with you is like and they can spread the word much more effectively than strangers can – *but you have to ask for their help.*

Summary

- Most people know around 250 people, who each know 250 people – you probably know more people than you realize
- Concentrate on finding people who can refer clients to you
- It's OK to ask for help and your coaching practice will get going faster if you do
- Networking works well for coaches because it allows you to meet face-to-face with prospective clients and people who could refer clients to you
- There are lots of different types of networking events available – choose those that will give you the best chance of meeting the kinds of people you want to work with
- When you're clear about your niche, find out where people like them get together – look for conferences, exhibitions and special interest groups as well as networking groups
- If you are leaving a job, make sure you leave on good terms and take your address/contacts book with you
- Be specific about what you want to achieve by networking otherwise you can waste a lot of time and money
- Are you a hunter or a farmer?
- Make a point of talking to the speaker if there is one – there may be opportunities for you to help one another out
- There are four deadly sins of networking – excluding people from conversations, hard-selling, monopolizing people and looking over people's shoulders when they are talking
- Your elevator pitch is a fast way of you communicating what you do, how you work and the type of clients that you want to coach
- People remember stories – be ready with a relevant success story
- Your business card is an essential piece of kit – but make sure that it represents you well when you're not there. How do you want people to perceive you?
- Following up is often missed by networkers who sit back and wait for people to call them. Be proactive

- When choosing where to network think not only about who will be there, but what frame of mind they are in. Are they going to be receptive to what you're saying?
- It's all about quality rather than quantity. It's better to get to know a smaller group of key people well than know thousands of people who can't remember *your* name when you meet them
- Use feedback forms to constantly review and improve your performance as a coach as well as gathering testimonials and success stories
- Almost seven out of ten coaches don't ask their clients for feedback – they're missing out
- Your clients will give you referrals, but you need to ask for them

chapter seven Public Relations (PR)

SEVEN Public Relations (PR)

PR is one of the most effective ways of marketing yourself and your practice to a large audience. Because, not only is independent editorial coverage trusted by clients more than straight advertising, but it's almost free!

Good PR really can establish you as a recognized expert in your field or your niche, and it helps you to build up trust and credibility with potential clients. PR is anything that puts you in front of the *right* kind of people, getting your message across in the way that you want to.

And I think that that's the part that is absolutely key. You can get PR and public speaking engagements (Chapter 8) fairly easily, if you know what you're doing.

But you can end up giving out the wrong messages if you're communicating with the wrong people, or you're presenting yourself in a way that doesn't fit with your personal brand and how you want to be perceived by the people in your chosen market.

Getting featured in the press

The first step, before you pick up a pen to write a press release or start tapping on your keyboard, is to do your research.

Speak to people who are in your niche to find out:

- What they read
- What they *don't* read
- When they read it
- Where they read it
- Whether it is a physical publication or a virtual (online) one

Once you know what they're reading, you can start to read it yourself. I would recommend that you read the same press as your target clients for at least three months. This will give you:

- A good understanding of their issues/challenges
- Knowledge of what's going on in their world
- A sense of what the journalists like to write about
- Who currently writes on subjects like yours
- The tone of the publication – serious, tongue-in-cheek, controversial, etc.

When you have this information, you'll be able to write press releases and articles that are topical, relevant and interesting, plus you'll know exactly which editor or journalist to send them to, e.g. the features editor.

Be bold!

Once you know who to talk to, get in touch with them! Ring up and say you'd like to tell them about an idea for a story and ask if it's a good time to talk. Always ask, because if they're on a deadline, it's easier to say they're not interested in the story than it is to listen. When it's OK to talk, you should be able to get across the main aspects of the story in less than 30 seconds (like your elevator pitch). They get people pitching to them all day, every day, so make it interesting enough to stand out.

Have a press release ready to send to them, that is a one page document giving them all the essential info they need to know to decide whether to use the story.

Topical versus timeless

Some stories will be interesting at any time. Some will have a 'sell-by' date. Those with a sell-by date are the ones that are referring to a current TV show, an event or news story. When you're planning to send out a press release or an idea for an article, think about whether it's topical or timeless. If it's topical, it needs to arrive in time to be published while the story is still hot. Arriving one day after a story's sell-by date is no good to the journalist, their readers or to you. Timeless stories can be published at any time and will still be relevant.

Glossy monthly magazines plan their stories months, if not years in advance and it's usual for them to start working on an issue six months before it's due to go on sale. Weekly magazines and weekly and daily newspapers will plan themes months in advance, but journalists may not finish writing the articles until a week or two before they are published. It's much easier to have a topical article featured in a weekly magazine or newspaper. (News stories are written as the news comes in.)

Timings for glossy monthly magazines

Take note if you're planning to send topical press releases and articles to glossy monthly magazines. If you want to have articles on career change or weight loss featured in the New Year issue, you need to plan ahead.

The magazine on the newsagents' shelves on New Year's Day will probably be the February issue, which will have been on sale since the end of December. Back in June, if not before, the editor will have signed-off the themes of the monthly features for at least the next six months. While the magazine will be sent to the printer around the beginning of December, most journalists will have decided exactly what they're writing about a month or two before then. If you send a New Year's press release in December, you've missed the boat.

You can get a 'Forward Features' list from the advertising department of the magazine that will tell you what's been planned and when the deadlines are.

What is 'news'?

News is something that's new. It's something that's different and that people will be interested to read about, so it can include launches, announcements, recent success stories and controversial comment.

On its own, the fact that you're a coach may not be enough to get a story written about you. If you send a press release about that alone, you can expect to get a call from the advertising department to find out whether you want to do an ad. If you want editorial, you need an 'angle'.

Your angle could be:

- Your book has just come out
- You're doing a book signing at the local bookshop
- You've just helped someone to achieve an amazing feat
- You're running a workshop that they'd be interested in
- You've got something to say that might rattle some cages
- You're the only coach to specialize in ___________
- Your survey has just revealed that ______________

Put yourself in the journalist's shoes. They receive hundreds of press releases and e-mails each day from people pitching stories to them. The majority of them are plain boring, but some stand out as stories that their readers would find interesting.

Volunteer yourself as a resource

In addition to supplying journalists with articles and press releases, you can get interviews by offering your services as an expert on a particular issue.

Personally, I have been featured in a number of publications because I sent the features editor an e-mail offering help and setting out in bullet point form the topics I had information about, and what kind of help I was prepared to offer. One in particular called me that day for an interview as it would help him finish an article. The key with this kind of approach is to keep it short and to the point. If you've done your research you'll know who writes on what and what they're interested in.

Don't worry too much if you don't hear anything back for a couple of weeks, because editors and features editors get so much information sent to them that it's impossible to reply to everything straight away. Even the editors that I write for regularly and who know me well can sometimes take a week or more to respond to e-mails.

Be a big fish in a small pond

It's easier to get something featured in some of the smaller titles because they're hungry for content. Some of the small business magazines and some of the other trade and specialist magazines don't have a budget to pay freelance journalists to write for them. They rely on free contributions from people like you.

And that's where you can really maximize your opportunities for getting editorial because you're helping *them* out because you're giving them an article. They're helping *you* out because you're getting all this extra exposure for free.

Make a point of getting in touch with the specialist publications that people in your niche read. If your target clients are likely to be members of a club or other membership organization, find out whether they have a members' magazine. You'll have more success being featured in the members' magazine than a national newspaper or magazine. You can multiply your success even further if you're a member of that organization yourself because you're 'one of them'.

Haunted press releases

There are ghosts at work in the PR profession and they can help you to contact the 'other side' (clients and journalists). What I'm talking about are ghost writers. These are freelance writers who write articles for you but have your name as the author. Perhaps you don't feel confident writing or you simply haven't got the time to do it; in either case, the ghost writer can take on the project for you and come back with the finished article or press release, ready to be sent out by you.

Another alternative is to get a PR consultant to write for you and contact the media on your behalf. They already know people in the media and may be able to call in a few favours to get your name widely publisized.

In order to give the ghost writer or PR consultant a better understanding of what you want from them, you need to give them a *brief*. This can either be verbal or written, but you'll get the best result if you provide them with a written record of what you want so that they can refer to it.

It's also useful to focus your mind and use as a reference when you're doing your own PR. Here is an example of a brief for a press release.

Date for the press release
1st July

Desired publication date
15th July – end of August

Type of publications being targeted and location
Weekly professional magazines and trade journals for people working in marketing in the UK

Type of coaching being promoted
Career coaching

Objective – What do you want the reader to think, feel, do, etc.?

- It's normal for busy people to think about their career while they're on holiday
- They're not alone in feeling over worked
- This coach seems to understand people like me

I'd like them to visit the website and sign-up for a free report on Career Coaching for Marketing Professionals.

Theme/suggested title
Career Crisis

Target audience
Male and female professionals aged 25-35 working in marketing jobs across the country. Job titles would include: Marketing Manager, Head of Marketing, Marketing Director, Account Manager and Account Director. They would probably have some experience of managing other people and dealing with senior management in other departments.

Benefits of this type of coaching
Helps them to discover if they're in the right role and if not, to find a job that truly fulfils them. They can speak to an independent person, confidentially about their career before they make any major decisions. This means that they know they're doing the right thing before they decide to stay put, go for a promotion, ask for a pay rise or hand in their notice. They can also speak to someone who understands the pressures of their job and will help them find ways of managing themselves and their staff even better.

Special offer
There's a free report available on my website.

What's special about you?
I used to be a marketing director and have coached lots of ambitious people in marketing to make positive changes and good career choices.
Tone of voice Understanding, professional, but still with a sense of humour.
Number of words required 250
Note to Editors John Smith is a coach specializing in helping ambitious marketing professionals to get the job they deserve. Prior to becoming a coach in 2001, he had a successful marketing career which included senior positions at Virgin, Coca-Cola and Heinz.
Contact details Please include my name, company name, website address, phone, mobile phone and my e-mail address.
Any inserts to be included with the press release Summary of what's included in the free report
Method of distribution E-mail and post
Media list Marketing Week, Marketing, Campaign
Deadline for first draft of press release 10th June
Deadline for sign-off of press release 20th June

Broadcast media

If you are planning to promote yourself via radio or TV, it's worth investigating what media training is available in your area. Even the most confident presenters can freeze when they're put in front of a microphone or camera, so this will increase your confidence in dealing with the media – especially when it's live and you don't get any second chances!

Good training will also help you to think about creating sound bites that are very short phrases (even just a few seconds long) and key points that you can use when you're being interviewed.

Depending on what you're featured on, you may find that your 10-minute interview is cut to 20 seconds, so be sure that you can get your point across concisely. This is especially important if you're likely to be doing a lot of interviews, for example to support the launch of your latest book.

A case of mistaken identity

A gentleman called Guy was sitting in reception at the BBC. He had come for a job interview for a role in IT. When someone came into reception and asked for 'Guy', he got up and followed them. He thought it was a little strange when he was taken into a BBC News 24 studio and set up with a microphone, but assumed it was part of an elaborate recruitment process and didn't want to risk his chances by saying something. Before he knew it, he was being interviewed live on air about downloading digital music files from the internet. The interview was broadcast around the world.

It was only later that they realized he wasn't who they thought he was. They had been expecting a music specialist also called Guy.

Getting your own radio show

A number of coaches have managed to get regular shows on their local radio station, in some cases just by being bold enough to ask! There are benefits to approaching your local station:

- It's only listened to by local people, so you know it's focused on your immediate area
- They may not have a huge budget for paying presenters, so you could get a foot in the door by doing a freebie
- It's easier to get onto local radio than the regional or national radio
- It can be a huge boost for your profile – people you meet when you're out networking could be fans!
- Imagine if you could put recordings of your shows on your website for people to listen to – do you reckon that would give you credibility?

Following up your PR

OK, so you've managed to get yourself featured in a specialist magazine that all your prospective clients would read. Should you clear your diary and get ready for the phone to ring constantly?

Maybe.

There are so many factors to whether your editorial feature will generate the interest that changes your life:

- How many people read it
- Whether they're interested in it
- Whether they're ready to do something *right now*
- What else was featured in that issue
- Whether your contact details appeared correctly
- Did you give them a reason to call you *today*?

Even if the phone doesn't start ringing straight away, it certainly doesn't mean all is lost. Because I haven't told you about the *real* secret to PR. Do you want to know what it is?

Hmm ... OK then, I'll share. The *real* secret is that it's what *you* do next that counts.

Let's say that your ideal clients are widget salespeople and you've just had an article published in *Widget Weekly* about how removing their limiting beliefs can help them to achieve their sales targets and earn more money.

The widget salespeople might have been out on the road or too busy to respond to your article. You could sit back and wait for the phone to ring or you could send a copy of the article to the sales managers of all the widget companies. The covering note or letter could tell them about how you work with widget salespeople and casually mention that you write for *Widget Weekly*. It establishes you as the expert in your field.

Then you ask the magazine to send you a pdf (portable document format) file containing the page that has your article on it. You upload it to your 'In the News' section of your website, then send an e-mail out to your database of widget salespeople, with a link to the article.

You contact the Widget Association and mention that you write for *Widget Weekly*. You ask about opportunities to speak at their events. As the 'widget sales expert' they book you there and then for a conference next month. They say they can't pay you, but the exposure should be good.

You send another note out to the sales managers inviting them to meet with you at the conference and send an e-mail to your database inviting them to book a ticket at the conference – telling them that you'll be speaking there.

By the time the conference comes around, the widget salespeople and the sales managers have already heard from you several times, plus, when they received their ticket, it came with a conference brochure that had your photo and biography in it.

They eagerly await your talk on 'How to Smash Your Sales Targets' and when you finish, they can't wait to shake your hand and pass you their card – in exchange for a free report on limiting beliefs. You have a stack of cards and quickly input them into your laptop in the break, firing off e-mails with the attached free report so that they will be there when the salespeople and sales managers get into the office the next morning.

In the bar later you get chatting to the US Sales Director of Widgets Global Inc. and he asks whether you'd consider coming to their New York office to deliver the talk to their top sales people. He also lets slip that the UK Sales Director is new to the role and Head Office has considered whether an executive coach might help – would that interest you? As if you need to think about it!

And it all started with a press release.

'Show me the money!'

We've been talking a lot about press releases, now it's time for you to create one of your own. Get your pen and paper handy and I'll take you through the steps of writing a press release.

A press release is a one (maximum two) page document sent to journalists to give them an idea of how they could write a story or article about you. Because of the time pressures placed upon them, journalists will typically look for stories that involve the minimum amount of effort on their part. So, if you've done the hard work for them by giving them a snappy headline, a story that they consider 'newsworthy' and interesting to their readers /viewers/listeners, with some comments or statistics that they can use, they are more likely to follow up on it.

Date

Always include a date! Otherwise how is a journalist supposed to know how long a release has been sitting in their in-tray?

Headline

This should grab their *attention*. Journalists receive many, many press releases each day and they will sometimes judge a press release on the headline alone. A successful headline appeals to the reader/viewer and is *newsworthy*. Put yourself in the journalist's shoes for a moment and think about which of the following headlines is easier to slot into a lifestyle magazine:

- Ann Jones has just started a life coach practice
- New research reveals the top ten reasons why women don't get the promotion they deserve – Ann Jones reveals all!

There are a number of effective styles of headline:

- **How to** – e.g. How to get the raise you deserve ... without having to hand in your notice to get it
- **Numbers** – e.g. 7 steps to getting more time with your family
- **What every** – e.g. What every sales manager should know about their team before launching a new product
- **New** – e.g. New e-book reveals how to you can start your own business in less than 6 months

EXERCISE

Write some headlines that would work for your niche.

Sub-heading

This should expand on the headline, perhaps with questions that will spark their *interest,* e.g. Do you long to start your own business, but worry about giving up your regular income?

EXERCISE

Now write some sub-headings that would work for your niche.

Main body of the press release

This is where you tell the story. If you have facts and figures to back up what you're saying, include them and state the source.

Remember, write as if you are a reporter. Try not to write in terms of 'I' or 'we' and don't make it too sales orientated. If there's something that you want to say, such as you're promoting what's special about your service, consider quoting yourself, e.g.

Ann Jones, founder of ABC Life Coaching, says *"Our service is second to none. We pride ourselves on delivering first class coaching packages to our clients. Our clients acknowledge that by recommending us to their friends and business associates. That's why we have been able to build our reputation through word-of-mouth."*

It's really important to write using the type of language that the readers/listener/viewer would use. If you're writing for a trade publication, use industry jargon or abbreviations. But only if you are sure that everyone reading it will understand what you mean! If you're not sure, use the term in full the first time you use it, showing the abbreviation in brackets. It's OK to use the abbreviation from then on.

EXERCISE

Write down some ideas on what you can put into the main body of your press release.

Notes for editor

This is where you include background information about you that isn't directly relevant to the story, but helps to build your credibility. For example:

Ann Jones is a professionally qualified Life Coach and specializes in Career Coaching. Her corporate clients include the BBC, The Times and Channel 4. She has appeared on Richard & Judy and writes the Career Coaching column for the trade magazine *Widget World*. She runs regular workshops to help female senior managers break through the glass ceiling.

EXERCISE

Write your 'notes for editor'.

Contact information

You'd be surprised the number of people who forget to include this in their press release! Usually if a press release sparks a journalist's interest, they'll call you back or e-mail you to arrange a time for an interview. You should include every means of contacting you possible – and *be available*! Remember to include your landline number and mobile phone number, your e-mail address and website address.

Summary

- Public relations includes anything that puts you in the public eye
- Start by being clear about what your clients read and don't read, then find out exactly who writes on your topic
- Is your story topical or timeless?
- Glossy monthly magazines plan several months in advance – you need to, too
- It's easier to get coverage in a smaller, more specialist magazine or a local paper than it is to appear in the national newspapers
- You can enlist the help of a ghost writer or a PR consultant to write your press releases and articles. They will need a brief from you
- There are media training courses available that will teach you how to make the most of radio and TV
- Getting an article published isn't the end goal – getting clients is. What can *you* do to make sure that everyone sees your article?

chapter eight Public Speaking

- Which speakers they have used before
- Which speakers they liked and which speakers they didn't like
- Which topics they liked
- What style they like

You'll find that there are some groups of people who will turn up to a 'workshop', but expect a formal PowerPoint presentation. There are also others who will turn up to a workshop and expect you to be getting people out of their seats, writing on flip charts and for it to be very interactive. If people have come with the wrong expectations in mind, it can be a little bit unsettling for them. So, do your background research with the event organizers to find out what their expectations are, so that you can meet those expectations.

Now it's time to plan your talk.

Title – once you've chosen your topic, create a punchy title for it, something that grabs their attention and makes them realize that it's for *them*. This title might be used on the organizers' website, in their adverts and sent out to their members in letter form.

Duration – how much time have you been allocated, and how much is available for questions and answers?

Exercises – do you have time to include some practical exercises that will get people involved and engaged in your talk?

Props and equipment – will they be providing flip charts, pens, laptop and projector, or will you need to bring your own?

Numbers – how many people will be coming? Make sure you've got enough handouts and business cards for everyone. Will your exercises work with big *and* small groups?

Self-promotion – will you be permitted to promote your coaching practice throughout the talk? Can you sell products at the end?

Public speaking nightmare!

Sometimes people are late arriving and the organizers delay starting an event until everyone is there. Unfortunately this usually means that they cut down the amount of time for each of the speakers and your hour-long presentation might be slashed to 35 minutes. Not good news – especially if you can't reduce your talk down and have to take the time out of your 'close' where you ask people to make a commitment by buying or signing up for something. You'll lose sales.

A solution is to break your talk down into sections and mentally mark them as either 'essential' or 'nice to have'. It's a good idea to time each section so that you know how many minutes you can make up if you're forced to cut one of them out.

Know your outcome

Before you set foot on the platform, be clear about why you're there. If you are there to gather details for an opt-in mailing list, everything in the talk should be leading up to people giving you their contact details. If you want to get clients to sign up for a free consultation, then everything should be leading towards that.

Don't make the mistake of thinking that if you show up, give them a nice talk and leave them feeling all warm and fuzzy inside, people will instinctively know how to take the next step. You have to take them by the hand and tell them what you want them to do. They then have the choice to either do it, or not. Either way, they've *done something*.

Opening well

It's a good idea to write an introduction for yourself so that one of the organizers can read it out before you come on. Many event organizers are nervous about standing up in front of groups and having something written out for them can stop them clamming up, waffling or even saying something that you'd rather they didn't. You can also use the introduction to establish yourself as the expert without appearing big-

on the day, you could follow up with a phone call (refer back to Chapter 6 on networking).

Personally, I have a much better sign-up rate from people who have seen me speak and then had my newsletter, than from people who have found my website and signed up for my newsletter. When people have seen you speak, they feel like they know you and it really does position you as a credible expert in your field.

Record your talk

It's easier than ever to record yourself presenting and then produce it as a CD that you can sell or give away. Most MP3 players have a record function on them and you can buy a lapel microphone very cheaply that will feed into the recorder. You can edit your talk on your computer and then either upload the file to your website or burn it onto CDs. Be aware that if you record the file as an MP3 and then burn it onto disk as an MP3, it will only work on a computer – not in a normal CD player. To get it to work, you need to create it as a .wav file. This is a much bigger file than a compressed MP3 file.

The next time you present the talk, you could sell CDs of you speaking live somewhere else. It's a good take-away and when people listen to it again, it helps them to know and trust you.

Audio CDs can actually appeal to all three modalities if people have seen you speak before – they can listen to you and remember what you looked like and how you made them feel, all at the same time.

More about modalities

Some people learn by looking at charts and images. Others like to listen to the speaker to understand the meaning behind what's being said. Others take in information experientially through exercises and role-play. Try to incorporate something for everyone in your talks and ensure that there's something to take away for the people who like to see and hold things.

Did you know the best time to sell someone a workshop is when they're sitting in another workshop? This is because they've already indicated – by showing up! – this is how they like to learn.

Did you know that the person who buys a CD from you is more likely to want to buy another CD (rather than a book) from you for the same reason?

Taking questions and answers

Depending on your style, you may welcome questions throughout your presentation or ask people to keep them to the end. Remember that not everyone is comfortable asking questions in front of other people and you should make yourself available *after* the talk to speak to people individually. If you do, you have a much greater chance of making those people feel special and they are more likely to become your clients if you spend a few minutes with them.

It goes without saying that you should know your material and only speak on topics that you are comfortable answering questions on. If you really don't know your topic well, it will show – especially if you're in a room full of people who know the topic better than you do.

Occasionally there will be a question from the audience that's from someone who thinks *they* ought to be up on stage talking about that subject. What they'll tend to do is when you ask for questions at the end, they'll say, *"Well, it's not so much a question – but a comment..."* What they're doing is trying to show that they know more than you do and they'll do this by turning to the audience to address their comments to them – not to you. This is sometimes followed by a difficult question, designed to 'catch you out'.

Make sure that you acknowledge the person asking the question by saying something like, *"What a fantastic question, I'm really glad you asked that."* Provided you know the answer, this is your opportunity to say so. If you don't, you have a choice: you can either admit that you don't know the answer or ask the audience what they think and allow some discussion amongst the group.

Avoid confrontation in front of an audience and keep the tone friendly and approachable. If you've handled the situation well, you'll usually

Taking questions and answers

- Record your talk by using an MP3 player or other recorder
- Be prepared for challenging questions from the audience
- Make sure that you create the right impression through the outfit you choose

chapter nine Getting Started on the Internet

end of that broadband or dial-up connection, there's another *real person* who is looking for services in the same way that people have looked for services for years – they make decisions based on what is attractive to them and what seems to meet their needs.

Depending on your target clients and how much time they spend online, only you can make a decision on whether having a website is an essential part of your marketing toolkit, or if it's simply something that's nice to have. A good test is how actively people like your target clients look for services similar to yours on the internet. My own experience and research tells me that people use the internet in different ways, depending on the context:

Personal coaching – people use the internet to look for coaches in their local area. This is because many people still don't know that coaching can be conducted over the phone, and even if they do, many want to meet their coach once or twice before trying telephone coaching. When searching for a coach online, they will check out several sites before finding someone who looks/feels/sounds right.

Business/corporate/executive coaching – decision-makers such as company directors, partners or HR/learning and development professionals are approached by coaches several times a week so don't generally go out looking for coaches. They mostly use the internet to check for the credentials and experience of the people who they have already met/been approached by.

Of course, there are exceptions and I've been approached by businesses who have found my company through an internet search and I've had personal clients who have met me first, then checked out my credentials. The examples I've given are a guide to how most people use the internet. Through your own research, you'll find out more about your clients and how they like to search for and receive information.

There are a few reasons for you considering getting your own website:

1. Credibility

In the past people might have asked you to 'send them a brochure', now they're more likely to ask for your website address so that they can find out more about you.

Having a website can improve your credibility, especially when you use it to demonstrate how good you are through:

- Credentials – usually the 'About us' page includes your qualifications, background and could include a mini CV
- Testimonials – what your clients have said about you
- Client lists – who you typically work with, for business/executive coaches you could include the names of companies you've coached in
- Press articles – the articles you've had published about you
- Video/audio clips – they can see and hear you talking about coaching or even coaching a client (you'll have asked their permission to record the session first!!). You could also include a clip of you presenting a workshop or seminar
- E-books and downloads – free reports, tips booklets, etc
- Other products – audio CDs, DVDs, etc.

The website is there to reassure the person looking at the site that they've come to the right place and you are the coach for them.

EXERCISE

If you were going to hire a coach to help you get your practice started, what would you want to know about them from their website before you got in touch? How would you know that they could do the job effectively? What would reassure you that they were the coach for you?

2. Providing resources for your clients

It may be that you want to have a website where clients can go into a particular section and download different files and tools that you will be using in your coaching sessions with them. Some coaches put a 'Wheel of life' on their website to help prospective clients to identify the area that they'd like to work on first.

You can use your website to provide prospective clients with other hints and tips free of charge to help them to get a sense of whether they would work well with you as a client. For example, you can go to: www.marketinghelpforcoaches.com and sign-up to receive free marketing tips, especially for coaches.

3. Selling products and services

Did you know that you can create downloadable books and audio/video files and sell them on your site? In addition to helping to establish yourself as a credible expert in an area, you can create an alternative income stream for yourself. This helps you to escape from the 'hours for money' trap. You could be earning money from your website when you're sleeping, walking the dog or coaching other clients.

4. Vanity

I'm serious! Some people want to have a website...because they want to have a website about them. If this is you, that's absolutely fine by me, but do me a favour and just be honest with yourself about why you're putting a website together. Vanity websites rarely impress anyone but you. Why? Because they've been designed with *you* in mind, not your clients. If you want your website to bring you clients and make you money, think about your client first and foremost – what will they want to know and how can you use your website to build a relationship with them?

How much does a website cost?

You can spend as much or as little as you want on a website. You can easily get a web presence for under £100 (approx. $185) or you can just as easily spend up to £5,000 (approx. $9,300).

But you really don't have to spend a fortune on websites. There are ways that you can have yourself a website presence without needing to have a website of your own. Now, what do I mean by that? Well, one option is to start blogging.

JARGON ALERT!

Blog – short for weblog and is an online journal that is updated frequently and anyone can read. Blogs can be used to comment on the news, publish articles, update the world on your exploits, educate your prospective clients about what you can do for them and subtly promote your coaching practice.

Blogger – someone who 'blogs'.

Blogging – the act of writing a blog.

There are a number of free sites where you can start your own blog. Put 'free blog' in your search engine to find one.

Readers of your blog can reply to your comments and post comments of their own. Usually this is a great way of getting your readers and prospective clients involved, but it has been used by spammers who post links to their own websites in the comments sections of unsuspecting bloggers. You can put restrictions on whether you have to see and approve the comment before people go on. It also ensures that no one puts anything you wouldn't want to be associated with on your blog. In addition, if people like your blog and want to be kept up-to-date with any additions, they can sign up to be notified when you add articles.

Another way to get a web presence without having your own website is to post your details on the online networking websites (search for 'online business networking' through your search engine). All of them allow you to put your profile, logo, photo and a description of what you do for other online networkers to see.

Some sites allow you to post things in discussion rooms and give you a blog as well. What's good about these sites is that as well as getting yourself known by other members of the network, you could find what you post featuring highly on search engine results. Because people all around the world are adding to the site every minute of every day, the search engines pick up on any changes very, very quickly – more quickly than they would if you had your own site. Some of the major search engines can take up to six months to visit a new website, but if you post something on a blog or on an online networking site, it's going to get looked at by the search engines within a matter of days, so people will start to find you.

Depending on who you did your coaching training with, you may be entitled to a free listing on their website. If you are a member of coaching organizations you may have the facility to put a listing on their site too.

There are lots of other options for getting yourself a free web presence – websites about your town or village, personal development websites, business websites – the list goes on!

EXERCISE

Write a list of all the places that you could get featured online without having your own website.

What do you want your website to do?

If you do decide that having a website is the right thing for you to do, the first question you need to be able to answer is: *What do you want your website to do for you? What is the outcome you want?*

'Get me clients' or 'make me money' is too wishy-washy. Come on, you're a coach – be specific!!

Do you want visitors to your site to:

- Pick up the phone and find out some more information?
- Download information that you've got on there?
- Sign up for an e-mail list so that you can continue to send them helpful messages?
- What else?

If you ask me, the number one priority is to get visitors to do *something*! The worst websites are the ones that are simply a brochure or 'vanity site' and don't tell the visitor what to do next. On *each page* of your website, there should be a call to action.

JARGON ALERT!

Call to action – the action that the marketer wants the prospect to take and usually uses a command in the text, e.g. enter your e-mail address here to download the free report; call this number to request a brochure.

But what 'something' should you get them to do? Something that moves them closer to becoming a client. The last thing you want is for people to visit your website and say, *"Oh, this looks interesting"* and then leave, and never come back again. The best possible result is that you have *their* contact details and their permission to get in touch with them. You can do this by giving them something free in exchange for their contact details. You could offer:

- Free report on something that they'd be interested in
- Free e-book or other download
- Free e-course delivered regularly into their e-mail inbox
- Free newsletter or ezine

JARGON ALERT!

E-book – an electronic version of a book, usually written in a word processing package and saved as a pdf file.

E-course – a multi-part course, usually delivered automatically over a period of days or weeks by e-mail.

Ezine – an electronic magazine or newsletter, usually delivered by e-mail.

Once you have someone's permission to contact them, you can start building a relationship with them and help them to understand what's special about what you can offer and why they should choose you. Remember, if it takes approx 5-7 communications from you to trust you enough to become a client, you need to get prospective clients to do more than visit your website ONCE.

If you're wondering how to capture people's contact details on your website or offer e-books, e-courses and ezines, never fear, there are packages that will take you through step-by-step how to set it up. If you go to www.marketinghelpforcoaches.com and go to the resources section, you can find some of the packages I recommend.

With most of them, you pay a monthly subscription and there are various online tutorials that will walk you through all the steps to setting up sign-up boxes, autoresponders, e-books and even give you customizable templates for your newsletters or ezines. They will even manage your 'unsubscribes' and bounces for you. Some incorporate a feature where you can check whether your e-mail would end up in the spam/junk-mail filter before you send it, allowing you to make changes so that it arrives exactly where it should – in the inbox.

JARGON ALERT!

Sign-up boxes – web-based forms that capture contact details and e-mail addresses and automatically add them to your database so that you can send them newsletters, ezines and autoresponders. The package you use will create the form as HTML for you or your webmaster to put into your website.

Autoresponder – en e-mail feature that sends out an automated e-mail message in reply. These are commonly used for 'out of office' replies, but can also be used to send out sequences of e-mails, such as e-courses as requested by your clients. You can time when the e-mails are sent out to people and the sequence that they receive them in

HTML – Hyper-Text Mark-up Language. The programming code that is used for writing most websites.

Unsubscribes – when recipients of e-mailed newsletters, e-courses and ezines notify you that they no longer wish to receive those messages. This can be dealt with manually where you have to remove them from your database, but can also usually be automated by including an 'unsubscribe' link in the e-mail itself if you use one of the newsletter/ezine packages.

Bounces – when you receive notification that an e-mail has 'bounced', i.e. it has not been possible for the e-mail to be delivered. Newsletter/ezine packages will keep a record of bounces so that you can check the contact details are correct.

Spam – repeated unsolicited e-mail, also known as 'Junk Mail' because the recipient has not asked for it. Spammers – the senders of spam – frequently use phrases such as 'FREE' and 'Click Here' in the body of the e-mail that can mean that your legitimate e-mail messages to clients can be wrongly filed as Spam/Junk Mail when they are received.

Getting the right keywords

Providing you've been doing all of the exercises in this book and you've researched your market, you should have a good idea of who you're targeting and what is going to really make them take notice of what's on your site.

Your keywords are the words that are going to appeal to your target market. They show the visitors that they've arrived in the right place – they've come *home*. It helps you to create rapport with your prospective clients, by using the kind of language that they use.

If your client is the kind of person who will use very formal language, then your website should reflect that. If they're going to be using very informal language – then do that on your website as well. Because, by using the wrong tone and by using the wrong words you can put people off without really realizing why.

You may also find that some people will use one phrase when they're searching online and other people will use another.

So your keywords will:

- Show the people that they're in the right place
- Build rapport with your prospective clients
- Help the search engines to *find your site and put you at the top of the search results.*

Let's say that you're coaching people on career change, you might consider using the following words in your website:

Career, change, redundancy, maternity leave, career coaching, advice, CV, resume, job interviews, interview technique, re-training.

Your main keywords should be in the meta-tags section of your webpage, the title of the webpage, as well as in the first few paragraphs of text to stand any chance of appearing high on search engine results.

JARGON ALERT!

Meta-tags – the section of HTML code, that isn't visible to site visitors, but tells the search engines what the page is about.

EXERCISE

Write down all the words associated with the kind of coaching you want to do and the words that your prospective clients might use to search for you online.

Use testimonials and case studies

You already know that testimonials and case studies help your prospective clients to understand how you can help them. When you did the exercise earlier in this chapter about what you would want to know about a coach before you hired them, I'm willing to bet that one of the things you'd look for was evidence that they'd successfully coached someone like you before.

Given that testimonials are so powerful, it would be a crime against coaching, not to include them on your website because your clients will find them so helpful. Many coaches put their testimonials together on a separate page of their site. While this is helpful from a navigation point of view – it helps people to find them – sometimes people don't consciously look for them. I'd argue that there's benefit to putting a short (and I mean one or two sentences) testimonial on each and every page.

Tell people how to contact you

Just as it's good to put testimonials on every page, you should put your contact details on every page because you never know for certain where someone's going to enter your site – it's not always via the home page.

For example, the search engine might have picked up that your page three is the most relevant for someone when they're searching for certain keywords – if you don't have your contact details on that page, don't assume that they will click on the contact tab at the top or search around your site to try and find them – they might just leave.

You need to make it really easy for people to pick up the phone to you, or to send you an e-mail.

Whilst it's attractive to you to put a form on the website and get someone to fill in that form so you've got all their details, some people don't like doing that and they just want to pick up the phone and talk to a real person.

I had an experience of this where a researcher from a TV company got in touch with me simply because I was the only site they found that had a phone number on it. They needed to speak to a coach urgently and didn't want to wait for someone to respond to a request for info via a form. I've had press journalists get in touch with me on deadlines because they were frustrated that the coaches they normally talk to didn't give a phone number – you had to go through a form on their website or e-mail them.

Clients want to be coached by a person

It's tempting to have a fancy name for your coaching practice and talk in terms of 'we' the whole time, but take care that you give your prospective clients information of who YOU are on your website.

You don't have to include every tiny detail about your life including your pets' names and ages and whether you got a swimming certificate at school. Just include things that are relevant to your clients, such as whether you've got relevant qualifications, the types of people you coach and anything else that demonstrates that you've got experience and will give you credibility.

Does everyone know what coaching is?

Coaching is becoming more popular, but some of your prospective clients may be a bit muddled about what constitutes coaching and what doesn't. It's best to manage people's expectations up front and tell them what coaching is and what it isn't in very straight-forward terms. Make sure that somewhere accessible there's a 'What is coaching?' or a FAQs (Frequently Asked Questions) section. Remember, if you've got your keywords right, people might have arrived at your site because you can help with their issue, but they may not have heard of coaching before.

However, the job of your website is to get you clients, not to sell coaching generically. There are enough sites out there that are run by the training organizations that will tell people, in detail, what coaching is. Your site is there to demonstrate that you are the right coach for them. Make them understand that you are the coach who is *the best* coach for them and you're going to get the right results for them.

Should I include my rates on my site?

If you're coaching *personal* clients I would *strongly suggest* that you put your pricing on there. It positions you in the mind of the client and will help you to screen *out* the clients who can't afford you before they call and screen *in* the kinds of clients you want to work with. There's a saying that 'if you have to ask, you can't afford it'. If rates aren't on your site, prospective clients may be reluctant to contact you for fear that they'll be embarrassed when you talk about the price.

If you're pricing yourself at the high-end of the market, do you really want to be spending your time with people who are expecting to pay £20 a session? – Probably not. Putting your rates on the site also helps the people that *can* afford your rate to feel like you're the right coach for them because you're used to dealing with people at the higher end of the market.

Equally, if you're coaching at an introductory rate, you will then become attractive for the people who are on a budget.

Also put whether you've got any packages available. Tell them what's included in each package so they know exactly what to ask for when they do pick up the phone or get in touch in another way.

You might think, *"I won't put the prices on there so I can negotiate with them when we speak"*. Can I ask you something? How would you, as a client, react to that? Would you suspect that the coach might make up the prices on the spot? I'll be honest, putting prices on your site does mean fewer people get in touch, but the people who *do* get in touch are serious about it. I mean it, if you want to spend your time talking to tyre-kickers who have no intention of paying for coaching and dealing with rejection, then keep your prices off the site. If you want to talk to people for whom the price isn't an issue, put prices on your site.

The only exception is if you're coaching in environments where the coachee isn't paying the bill – their employer is. When an organization wants a quote for coaching, there can be lots of variables:

- Your travel time to and from the client's office
- The preparation work involved for each client
- How many people you'll be coaching
- At what level
- If it's a long-term, retainer contract

It's impossible to give website visitors an accurate quotation on your site. Even if you give them an hourly rate, would you still charge the same rate if they expected you to drive two hours to their office, coach one person for an hour, then drive two hours back? That's five hours away from your base and you'll be exhausted when you get back – you'll have to write off the whole day for one hour's work.

Are you coaching both individual clients and corporate clients? I strongly suggest that you have TWO websites – one for individuals and one for corporate clients. This ensures that the corporate clients won't be exposed to your rates for individual clients and expect to get the same rates. It also means that the tone and content of your site – the images and words you use – will be appropriate for the people visiting each site.

Get people engaged

Most websites are static and are designed for only one sense – sight. We know that different people use their senses in different proportions, so whilst most people have the use of their sight, not all use it as their primary sense. Even if people are mostly visual, it doesn't follow that they will all like to read things on their computer screen. Some people print things out, hold them and read them. Others like to listen and make notes. Others like to watch videos of people talking.

If you have something catering for all of the modalities (visual, auditory, kinesthetic) you increase the chances of people staying on your site and getting a sense of rapport with you. You could use:

- **Video** – you talking to camera, your satisfied clients talking to camera, you being interviewed, you coaching someone, you presenting a workshop, etc.
- **Audio** – you talking, your satisfied clients talking, a recording of a teleclass, interview or workshop
- **Photo** – portrait of you, 'action shot' of you and/or your clients

Disability access

When designing your website, make sure that it can be accessed by everyone. Blind, deaf and other disabled people use the internet as much as other people do and they have the right to access all the information publicly available on your website. Ask your website designer for more guidance on this.

You should also consider how you would coach someone who had a disability that prevented them from talking on the phone, accessing the premises you coach from or completing the exercises or 'homework' you set for them. Have a contingency plan, just in case.

If your clients have seen your photo, listened to your voice and watched you in action, it is much easier for them to have the sense that they know you and they like you. This will help you to stand out if they are going through lots of other coaches' sites.

Writing content for your website

The first place to start is to think about your niche – think about your client. Use their language and keywords. Write in a style that fits with their style – if they're formal, write in a formal way; if they're informal, write in an informal way. Are they the kind of people that will need a gentle approach, or will they be more responsive to a hyped-up salesy, energetic style of writing?

Also, if you're thinking about recording yourself talking on the website, think about what style of speech is going to appeal to people. Will they want something that's fast paced, *punchy*, exciting – or will they need something that's a little bit more subdued, gentle? Just take your time with them so you can explain what it's all about.

So all of this will help the people that are in your niche to understand that they are in the right place, and the best way to do that is to talk to a few people:

- People who are your clients already
- People who are prospective clients

Get them to have a look at what you're planning to put on your website. Get them to listen to you speaking on your website so that you can get some feedback from them before you go ahead with it all – because you might find that they say, *"Oh no! That's all wrong! That wouldn't appeal* ***at all!****"* And then you can save yourself some time, some money and some tears – because you can get it right, right from the start.

A couple of things to think about when you are writing the content: try not to talk about 'I', 'me' or 'our' all the time – use *'you'* much more than you use the word *'I'*, and talk in terms of what your client is going to get from it, more than what you offer them.

Think about what the benefits are rather than the features. If possible, write in the third person. When you're writing your 'About you' section

– write as if you were somebody writing about you, rather than *'I do this'* and *'I do that'* and *'I went to the university here'* and *'I coach...blah, blah, blah'*.

Write it in the third person because, hey! you can give yourself many more compliments when you make it sound like somebody else is writing it, compared to if it sounds like you're writing it yourself. But whatever you do, make it interesting, make it relevant.

How much should I write on my website?

Well, as my website designer said to me, *"You need to write about a third as much as you would if you were writing a brochure."*

This is because you've got a few seconds to grab peoples' attention. They don't really want to be scrolling down loads and loads of text. Break up long text into sections and have it on different pages so people can find the page that they're looking for and get just a short summary of the points that you need to get across to them.

Also think about using audio rather than a great big long piece of text – because it's much easier for somebody to sit back and listen to you talking than it is to read through loads and loads of information. This will help to build that relationship with you.

'Long copy sales letters' are best kept for selling products (e-books, audio CDs, etc) and seminar tickets, rather than one-to-one coaching.

Reinforce your call to action

When you're writing your contents, think again about what you actually want people to do. Because every word counts here. If what you've written on the site isn't driving somebody towards a desired outcome – it's just padding. You don't need padding on your website because people will get bored with it.

Getting the look right

Again, go back to your target market. Before you start using logo's, fonts, colours, images – who are you targeting and what's going to appeal to them?

Get the context right, because if you're offering life coaching, the same person who works in a high-powered job and wears suits every day but is looking for coaching on their 'me time', might be put off by photos of people in suits. And vice versa, a business coaching website with photos of people dressed in jeans and t-shirts playing with children might put people off because it doesn't 'look right'.

This is where understanding your prospective clients and what appeals to them is absolutely key. What do you want your website to say about your coaching practice? What is the message that you really want to get across in the images and the visuals that you use?

Even down to looking at the photo of yourself that you put on there. It's very tempting to just say, *"Ooh that's a nice photo of me taken at a wedding 15 years ago"* or *"I'll just grab my camera phone and get a shot for the website."*

Stop – because it's all about perception. If in that really nice photo you're holding a champagne glass and looking a bit squiffy – is that *really* the image that you want your clients to have of you? It might be a lovely photo and it might be really flattering, but is that the image that you really want to portray? That shot taken on your camera phone might be great – on your camera, but look amateurish on your website. Equally, it's easy to have a very formal, stuffy, professional portrait photo taken – when what would appeal to your clients is something that looks a little bit more relaxed and fun.

Do think about how you want your clients to perceive you. What does your image say about you? If you're not sure, you can always make an appointment to see a personal branding or image consultant who will help you. They can give you advice on what to wear, not only for your website photo, but when you're going to networking events and business meetings.

You may also want to use other photography on your site. Lots of coaches use inspirational or aspirational photos on there – that is great! But take care to choose images that are right for your clients. For example, if you're thinking about putting some things from nature on your website, you might like fluffy bunnies – but does everybody? You might be inspired by mountain scenes or people jumping out of aeroplanes – but those same images might fill somebody else with dread. You might have photos from a holiday or a trip around the world that you want to use, and they're very personal to you. But are they actually relevant to your client? Think about what is actually going to float their boat. What is going to get them really excited and make them feel that you're the coach for them? Taste is a very personal thing.

Are you planning on including photos of people on your site? The best option is to show images of the kind of people who are in your target market, because if you want to appeal to retired couples, there is no point putting a twenty-five year old, young and attractive woman on there. It's not going to help them to feel that you understand them.

Colour

The next thing to think about is the colour that you choose on your website. Would you believe that there is a whole psychology behind colour? Companies spend thousands, if not *millions*, on getting their branding absolutely right. Have you noticed that most fast food restaurants have got red in their logo?

The reason is that red is a very intense colour. It stimulates a fast heart-beat and rapid breathing, and it's also the colour that inspires you to feel hungry. If you snack a lot in the kitchen and you've got a lot of red in there – that could be why. The colour is actually stimulating you to eat more. I'll come onto some of the different colours soon, but there are four big considerations when you're thinking about colour:

1. Culture

If you're going to be trading globally, you need to think about what the colours mean in different cultures. In the western world, white is seen as a very clean, fresh colour – but in China it's the colour of death.

2. Considered purchase vs impulse buy

If you're trying to encourage people to buy on impulse, then go towards reds, oranges, blacks or blue. If you want to attract the people who plan ahead, they prefer colours like pink, light blue, navy. These are the colours that will attract people who *consider* things before they buy.

3. Status

Consider the status of your target clients – bright colours can appeal to people who are from a lower income, whereas the people who are in higher income brackets tend to use more classic and subtle colours.

4. Geography

In colder climates people seem to like colder and neutral colours, whereas in hotter climates, such as Latin America and Africa, people are more comfortable with brighter, much stronger colours.

The language of colour

Red	Energy, speed, danger and excitement
Blue	Trust and reliability
Yellow	Warm, stimulating, happiness, but also the colour of fear and betrayal
Orange	Warm, vibrant, encourages impulse purchase
Green	Fresh, cool, nature, growth and hope. But it can also be associated with illness and superstition
Purple	Royalty, spirituality and dignity
Pink	Soft and nurturing. Too much can be seen as childish
White	Purity, cleanliness. Death in Asia
Black	Sophisticated, up-market – especially when used with gold and silver. Can symbolize death and the occult
Gold & Silver	Prestige. Silver can be used to give something more of a scientific association

Style of writing

Let's have a think about the type that you'll use on your website, and I mean *Font* type. When you're designing your website, try not to use *italics*, all **bold** or all UPPERCASE, because they can be quite difficult to read.

Also try not to do reverse out type on a coloured background. What I actually mean by that is, if you had a red block for instance with blue text over the top of it – it can be a bit difficult to read. However, yellow highlighted individual words and phrases have worked on online sales letters because they bring the reader's attention to certain words.

Avoid putting text over images, logos or dancing graphics as it's confusing. Beware if your website designer wants to get carried away and use a lot of 'Flash' on the site. This can give you swooping graphics and animation, and it all looks very exciting – but the search engines have difficulty reading Flash and understanding what the site's about.

Another thing to bear in mind: don't put too little or too much space between lines. If you put too little space, it can end up looking really crammed. If you put too much space it becomes a bit laborious to read through and people can lose their place. Try to give people lists and bullet points wherever possible because it makes it a lot easier to read.

Justify things on the left-hand side of the page because it's a lot easier on the eye. If you start centering it on the page it can be a bit difficult and jumbled to read, and it can get messy when you try and make all of the line breaks line up.

How do you choose a website designer?

So you know why you've got the website, you've figured out what you want to put on there, you've got your keywords, you know the pages you're going to include, how you're going to write it, what you want it to look like – how do you find a good website designer?

The best thing to do is to ask somebody you know who has had a good website done, and find out from them who did it.

Of course, you can go to family or friends and have a website designed at a knock down rate. The problems come when you need changes done

– yesterday, and they don't have time or don't see it as being as urgent as you do. If something goes wrong or something needs doing very quickly, and you have to start putting your foot down it's a lot easier to be dealing with someone who you don't have an emotional connection with.

It's a horrible situation to be in when you have to 'have words' with friends or family – they can take it very personally.

DIY websites

Will you need the flexibility to change and update your website from time to time? If so, it's worth going to a website designer who set up your site with a *content management system*. This will allow you to make changes to the text, change photos and add pages yourself. It's all set up using a template, and you just need to type into the relevant section of the template and it will automatically update it and put it into your website in the right place. You don't need to know all about HTML or complex code to do it.

Many hosting providers offer free or cheap templates as part of the package you buy from them. You can buy good templates 'off-the-shelf' on the internet for about £30 – but you do need to know what you're doing, because if you want to do something that's outside of that template, it can be quite tricky to make changes. Also, many of them are intended for use with website design software which you may not have.

JARGON ALERT!

Hosting – storage of your website on a server. You pay a subscription to rent space on a server. Some hosting providers bundle other services such as templates and blog facilities into the package.

What's the difference between a website designer and a developer?

If you are going down the route of needing to get somebody else to develop your website for you – find out whether you're talking to a designer, or a developer.

The difference is that graphic designers are very good at making things *look good*, and developers are more involved in the functionality of a site.

Developers generally tend to be people who are a bit more savvy about internet *marketing* and will have a better understanding of SEO (*search engine optimization*).

JARGON ALERT!

Search engine optimization – adapting and altering the content, keywords and code of a website to improve its chances of appearing highly in the natural listings of the search engine results

Natural listings – the part of the search engine results that have not been paid for, usually the main section of the results

When discussing the price for building your website, find out what's included. Ask about:

- **Corrections** – do they include all corrections and amendments until the site is as you want it?
- **On-going changes** – will you have to pay extra if you want changes made at a later date?
- **Support** – what happens if there are glitches or you need other support to do with the site?
- **Domain name registration** – do you have to buy the domain name or will it be included in the price?

- **E-mail set-up** – will they help you to get your e-mail account set up?
- **Hosting** – can they host the site for you? If so, what's included?
- **Copyright** – who holds the copyright of the site – you or them?
- **E-commerce/shopping cart** – can they set up online payment systems for you?

JARGON ALERT!

Domain name – the unique name or address of a website, for example www.marketinghelpforcoaches.com

URL (Uniform Resource Locator) – the unique name or address of a website, including the protocol *http://* before the domain name, for example http://www.marketinghelpforcoaches.com

E-commerce – electronic commerce, the process of buying and selling via the internet

Shopping cart – a payment system that allows you to store one or more items in a 'cart' before paying for all of them in one transaction.

Choosing a domain name

It makes sense that if you're selecting a name for your coaching practice that you check online to see if anyone else has already set up a website using the name. If the .com version of the name is taken, you may still be able to get the .co.uk, .net, .biz, .eu etc version, BUT your prospective clients may end up on the other site by mistake. Wherever possible, try to get a name that's unique and is easy to remember.

Because the search engines look at the domain names for sites as well as the content of the site, it's a good idea to include coach or coaching somewhere in the name you choose. You could also include a keyword that describes what's on the site and who your clients are, for example www.marketinghelpforcoaches.com has keywords in the title and describes what's on the page.

If you are the main or only coach in your practice, consider using your name as the domain name. Do you have a common name? Think about variations by combining your name with the type of coaching you do.

Selling products via the internet

In order to sell products from your website or to allow people to book and pay for coaching sessions online, you'll need to set up a means of taking payments. In most cases, this means getting a 'merchant account' so that you can take credit card payments. You can either do this through your bank or by using many of the accounts available online (search for *merchant account*). To set up a *shopping cart* system, you will need to have a merchant account.

For some providers, go to www.marketinghelpforcoaches.com and go to the resources section.

Getting people to look at your website

When did you last look for 'life coaching' through a search engine? The chances are that when you did, you found several million sites and the number is growing on a daily basis. It's great that people are talking about coaching online so much, but it does make getting your site to the top of the natural listings a bit of a challenge!

Relying on the search engines to get traffic to your site is becoming riskier and riskier, because with so many sites in existence – *it's hard to get right up at the top*. What a lot of the search engines have started doing is offering you *pay per click* advertising. You'll have seen them at the top and down the sides of the natural listings.

The way it works is that you write a short advert and then place a bid – how much you're prepared to pay to appear on the results for certain keywords. The advertiser that is prepared to pay the most for the ad gets first position. The next person gets second position and the amount that you pay is adjusted according to how many other people are bidding on that keyword. You can save money and get more targeted results if you bid for specific keywords and phrases that your target clients would be looking for, rather than very general words to do with coaching. You can also select the search terms that you *don't* want your ad to appear next to, for example 'soccer coaching'. You don't pay anything until someone clicks on your advert and is re-directed to your website, but you do need to keep an eye on how much you're spending compared to how many new clients you get as a result.

So, if you don't want to go down the route of pay per click advertising or trying to get your website to the top of the search engines, what else can you do?

Well, you can include the people who you meet networking on the distribution list for your newsletter or ezine and when you send it out, include links to new sections and articles on your website. With many newsletter/ezine providers, you can even track who has opened your e-mail and then clicked on a link.

If you like writing, you can post articles on free ezine and newsletter websites. Other people can use your articles in their own websites and ezines free of charge in return for crediting you for writing the article and including your contact details, and a link back to your website. Whenever your articles are published on other people's sites, you get an in-bound link to your site.

JARGON ALERT!

In-bound links – active links placed on other people's websites, that link back to your site. The more in-bound links to your site, the more important your site is considered to be by the search engines because other sites are suggesting that people visit your site.

Who do you know who is already sending out newsletters and ezines to their subscribers? There may be scope for a joint promotion where they promote you and your site in return for something. You could set up a formal 'affiliate programme' and give them a cut of any new business it generates or it could be a looser informal arrangement where you will return the favour at some time. Let's say you coach people around career and somebody else is coaching around nutrition and well-being. If you're not treading on each others' toes, you might be able to cross promote each others services to people on your list.

JARGON ALERT!

Affiliate programme – an advertising method whereby person A places a free advert on their site to promote person B's site in return for a share of the sales generated. Person A could also send out free promotional messages via their own newsletter or ezine encouraging people to visit B's site, again in return for a share of the sales generated. Person B pays person A on a commission-only basis, so it is an affordable marketing option.

You are still dealing with PEOPLE!

This chapter has been mainly about marketing on the internet, but it doesn't mean that your prospective clients will *only* search for information on the internet. You can drive people to your website through PR, including your website address on your business cards, in your e-mail signature, by giving people in your workshops a free download if they visit a certain page of your site or by offering a free e-course to people who sign up on your site – you could advertise it at the foot of all your e-mails. So it could be something like, *"Sign up for my ten top tips to a new brighter you"* so people will think ,*"Okay, well what's that? Let's go and sign up for it."*

Generally people won't register if you just put *"Sign up for my newsletter"* on your site because, most of us are getting so bombarded with information now, we don't need any more newsletters in our in-box. So make it something that's interesting. Don't just say, *"Sign up for my newsletter"*. You could say, *"Sign up to get my free download on 'X'; To get my free special report on 'Y'; To qualify for a free half hour Consultation"* – whatever it is that you want them to do.

Summary

- Before you hire someone to build you a website, be clear about why you want it and what you want it to do for you
- Individuals and organizations look at websites in different ways and for different reasons
- Every page of your website should contain your contact details and a *call to action*
- Capture people's details when they visit your site and you can continue to build a relationship with them via newsletters and auto-responders
- Use the keywords that your clients would use – this helps to build rapport and they will find you more easily via the search engines
- Testimonials and case studies can help you to build credibility
- Make your site interactive so that visitors get a sense of you and what it is like to be coached by you
- Unless you are selling seminar tickets or products from your site, keep the content simple and succinct
- Consider whether the image – including layout, images and colours – will appeal to your target clients
- When negotiating a price for building your website, find out exactly what is included in the price and whether you need to pay extra for corrections and on-going changes
- You can use pay per click advertising, online articles and other people's lists to drive traffic to the site

chapter ten Other Marketing Methods

TEN Other Marketing Methods

The previous chapters have given you quite detailed information about the types of marketing that tend to work best for coaches, but there are other methods you can use.

The best responses come from using a combination of different marketing approaches, for example, in the chapter on PR, you read about how a press release can lead you to all sorts of different opportunities.

Other options you could consider for marketing include:

- Advertising
- Direct marketing, sales letters, postcards
- Flyers, brochures, stationery
- Newsletters

How often should you promote yourself?

Many coaches run one or two adverts, send out a sales letter, make a few phone calls and wonder why they aren't drowning in new clients. The reality is that you need to be constantly marketing yourself.

The statement overleaf was written in 1885 by a man called Thomas Smith and it's as true today as it was then. Look carefully to see the point at which people will start to pay attention to a marketing message. Whenever you read the word 'ad' you can substitute it with 'sales letter', 'article', 'newsletter' or 'meet someone at a networking event'.

Marketing effectiveness

The first time a man looks at an ad, he doesn't see it.

The second time he doesn't notice it.

The third time, he is conscious of its existence.

The fourth time he faintly remembers having seen it.

The fifth time he reads the ad.

The sixth time, he turns up his nose at it.

The seventh time, he reads it through and says, *"Oh brother!"*

The eighth time he says, *"Here's that confounded thing again."*

The ninth time he wonders if it amounts to anything.

The tenth time, he will ask his neighbour if he has tried it.

The eleventh time he wonders how the advertiser makes it pay.

The twelfth time he thinks it must be a good thing.

The thirteenth time, he thinks it might be worth something.

The fourteenth time he remembers that he's wanted such a thing for a long time.

The fifteenth time, he is tantalized because he cannot afford to buy it.

The sixteenth time, he thinks he will buy it some day.

The seventeenth time, he makes a memorandum of it.

The eighteenth time, he swears at his poverty.

The nineteenth time, he counts his money carefully.

The twentieth time he sees the ad, he buys the article or instructs his wife to do so.

Advertising

In Chapter 9, we talked about *'pay per click'* advertising as an effective way of getting your message in front of people who are actively searching for information about the type of coaching you do. You could also consider using your local newspapers and magazines and the specialist newspapers and magazines that your target clients would read.

Before placing any paid-for print or broadcast advertising, consider how many booked client sessions you need to get to break-even on the advert. By break-even, I mean that the fees generated cover the cost of the advert (and everything associated with the advert, e.g. graphic design), your time in putting the advert together and any other costs involved in you delivering the coaching that comes from the sessions, e.g. room hire.

Remember, people may need to be exposed to your advert seven or more times to respond. So to get a good response, you may need to place an advert in the local paper for 7 weeks or in your local monthly magazine for 7 months before you start getting good responses. You have to be incredibly lucky to get a good response the first time you run an ad – repetition is key. You can use this as a bargaining tool with advertising salespeople and negotiate discounts for buying a series of adverts.

Until your ad is paying for itself, a small classified advert with a good call to action is probably all that you need. Make sure that it appears in the section that is most relevant to what you do and what your target clients are looking for. It's a bit like reading the horoscopes – people only look at their own star sign and ignore everything else.

When you did your research with the people in your target market, you'll have found out where they search for information.

Which of the following would your prospective clients search in?

National newspaper	Local newspaper	Trade newspapers
Business magazines	Specialist magazines	Lifestyle magazines
Internet	Notice boards	Supermarket boards
National radio	Local radio	Television

Once you've got some ideas on how to target your clients, there are a few questions that need to be answered:

- How many people read that publication or watch/listen to that show? Where could you find this information out?
- Are other coaches advertising in it?
- What are their adverts like?

If lots of other coaches are advertising in a particular magazine or paper, it's actually a good sign. People wouldn't keep advertising somewhere if it wasn't paying back. Think about your nearest town – are all the restaurants on the same street? Are all the furniture companies in the same area? Why do you think that could be?

Writing an advert

Unless you have a background in advertising, I would suggest that you get a professional to help you to design something that will appeal to your prospective clients and includes a call to action.

Here are some ideas you can use:

Headline – This should grab their attention. There are a number of effective styles of headline:

- *Is this you?* – e.g. Attention Single Mothers!
- *How to* – e.g. How to get the raise you deserve ... without having to hand in your notice to get it
- *Numbers* – e.g. 7 steps to getting more time with your family
- *What every* – e.g. What every sales manager should know about their team before launching a new product
- *New* – e.g. New e-book reveals how you to can start your own business in less than 6 months

Sub-heading – This should expand on the headline, perhaps with questions that will spark their interest: for example, do you long to start your own business, but worry about giving up your regular income?

Main body of the ad – Demonstrate how you're the solution to their problem. Make them **desire** what you can do for them. You could use testimonials, snippets from articles or the benefits of working with you. If you're writing for a printed advert, make it read like you're right there speaking to them. This is where you need to build rapport with them, so use words and phrases that they use and sound like you work with people like them all the time.

> **Some more tips:**
>
> **Tip #1:** Don't waste your time and money on a general advert saying what ***coaching*** will do for them, you've got to tell them what ***you're*** going to do for them. Otherwise you might persuade them that they need a coach, but then they go ahead and get coached by someone else!
>
> **Tip #2:** Use the word 'you' many more times than you use 'I'. People only want to know what's in it for them. They won't really care much about you until they know how much you care about them.

Call to action – This is where you tell them what you want them to do – tell them how to take action. If you give people too many options or don't make it clear what they need to do to take the next step, they won't do anything. There's a saying that 'a confused mind says NO'. Remember, you're unlikely to be the only coach out there and your ad might be next to someone else's who does give them a compelling reason to get in touch – who are they more likely to call? You owe it to your clients to get them to take action right now and take control of their situation. You're only prolonging their pain if you wait around and don't make them do something about it.

For example: E-mail me now on <insert your e-mail address> to get a copy of my free report 'The 7 secrets of successful actors'.

Or: Call me today on 000 000 0000 to book your coaching session. The first 5 callers get their first session absolutely free!

Direct marketing

This type of marketing is sent directly to the prospective client and can include letters, brochures (with covering letter), postcards and e-mails. Direct marketing can be used effectively to target business clients, but the direct marketing industry reports that a response rate of around 2% is standard – this means that for every 100 letters you send, 2 people might respond. Bear that in mind when you're working out how many new clients you need to get from a direct mail campaign.

You can increase your success rate significantly by sending more than one letter (remember, 5-7 communications before people begin to trust you) and by using other marketing methods, e.g. phoning them to follow-up.

In order to send a letter or any other type of mailing out to prospective clients, you need to know who they are and have their contact details. You could take them from your own database or buy a list of contacts from a list broker (search online for List Brokers). It's also possible to rent a list of members of a club/trade association or even the subscriber list of a particular magazine. If you have other business owners and/or coaches who you could do a joint venture with, they may agree to sending a letter out to the people on their database.

Once you have the list, think about where the recipient is going to be reading the letter. This is very important because the same person will be in a different frame of mind in different places, e.g. at home vs at work. For example, the same person may ignore a message about performing better at work if they receive it at home (and could regard it as an intrusion), yet be very receptive if they receive it at the office.

Some studies show that the best time for someone to read and take action on a mailer received at work is from Tuesday through to Thursday. Why? On Monday they'll be going through the post that arrived over the weekend and they'll spend less time reading each letter because there are more of them to go through and on Friday they'll either be winding down for the weekend or they'll be busy trying to get everything finished for the week. When do you need to *send* your mailer to ensure that it *arrives* on Tuesday, Wednesday or Thursday?

The actual content of direct marketing materials is similar to that of an advert (see above), but you have more space to explain yourself and you can personalize it by including their name. Many word processing packages allow you to do a 'mail merge' from a spreadsheet and you can also insert the person's name part way through the letter.

With any direct mail, be clear about how it fits into your overall strategy and how you'll follow up with the people who don't respond first time around.

Flyers and brochures

When many coaches start marketing themselves, they put a lot of emphasis on having a 'brochure' without thinking about what its purpose is. Indeed, when coaches start talking to businesses about coaching and they're asked to 'send some information in', they often start scurrying around trying to put an expensive glossy brochure together.

Remember, the clients are buying **you**. What is the best way for you to get across your personality and coaching style? Think creatively. For some people it will be a tri-fold flyer (A4 sheet folded into three sections), for others it will be an audio CD or even a DVD of them coaching someone. It needs to grab their attention and show that you're the right coach for them.

If you're not sure what will appeal to your target market, ask a few people and get some honest feedback. Find out exactly what they would need to see in a brochure/flyer/pack in order to make a decision on whether to take things further. If you are targeting more than one type of client, e.g. personal clients and corporate clients, then just as you should think about having two separate websites, you may need different printed materials for each group.

Stationery – letterhead and compliments slips

If you have a good colour printer, you do not necessarily have to go to the expense of having stationery professionally printed. However, you may find that if you're sending a lot of letters, for example sales letters to 250 people, it will end up costing you more in printer ink than you save! It may also take ages to print all those letters if you've got to print your own logo and contact details as well as the letter each time.

On your letterhead you should include:

- Company name/logo – if you are a limited company, you should state your full company name
- Address
- Phone number
- General enquiries e-mail address
- Website
- If you are registered as a limited company, you should have a line stating 'Registered in England No. <insert your registration number here>' and state your Registered Office

You should have the same information on your compliments slips, adding 'With compliments'.

If you are VAT registered, you only need to put your VAT Registration number on your invoices, so it's easier to overprint them onto your letterhead when you print your invoices out.

Newsletters

Newsletters are a great way for you to keep in contact with both your existing clients and your prospective clients.

Newsletters allow you to educate your prospective clients about what you do without being too sales-focused, but you must always remember **why** you are running a newsletter. The aim is to get clients!

A good newsletter, whether it's sent by post or e-mail should:

- Look professional
- Be interesting to read
- Address issues that are facing the reader
- Give the reader a good reason to get in touch with you
- Remind the reader who you are and what you do – a photo can help
- Include case studies or testimonials from happy clients to demonstrate that other people are using your services

- Be of a manageable size and frequency so that it doesn't become a chore to write
- Inform the reader of any events, seminars or workshops that you're running
- Always, always include your contact details!

It's a fine line between giving the reader enough information to get a good understanding of how coaching works, without it turning into a self-coaching tool. It's great to produce a newsletter that reads like a book on coaching, but if you do, what incentive is there for someone to hire you?!

Summary

- To get the best responses, marketing must be an on-going activity
- Advertising messages need to be placed repeatedly in order to build up a trusting relationship with your prospective clients
- Take care to make sure your ad appears somewhere where your clients can find it
- Include a heading, sub-heading, main body and call to action in advertising and direct marketing
- You can buy or rent other people's mailing lists if you don't already have your own
- Remember, get the context right so that the person receiving the letter is in the right frame of mind
- You don't need to spend a fortune on a brochure – find out from your contacts exactly what they'd expect from you
- Newsletters are good tools for educating your prospects about what you do and how you do it

chapter eleven Asking for the Business!

ELEVEN Asking for the Business!

This chapter is divided into two sections. The first is for people who are coaching individuals who are paying for coaching themselves. The second section is for coaches targeting organizations where the person paying the bill isn't always the person receiving the coaching. Even though it's split into sections, it's well worth reading both.

Section 1 Individual clients

You've started marketing and you've cleared time in your diary to coach....then someone gets in touch! It's make or break time! What should you do?

This can be the most nerve-wracking time for new coaches – speaking to prospective clients, talking about money and closing the deal. But if you have done your marketing well, this should be the most exciting part of running your coaching practice, as someone is giving you the opportunity to change their life.

Before we even think about 'selling', let's look at things from the client's perspective. We'll call that client 'Sarah' – here's her story:

For the past 12 months, Sarah hasn't been happy in her job. Her career path had been leading her up to this point and she'd finally got that promotion last year she'd been dreaming of. The trouble was that she'd also taken on more responsibility. For the first three months, she thought she was just settling in and put in some long hours to get everything done – she didn't want anyone to think she wasn't up to the job and she'd get 'found out'.

Then she started to notice that she hadn't spent much time with her friends. They were worried about her and said she had become a bit snappy. One even suggested going to a life coach – that was six months ago. Sarah had put it to the back of her mind – she didn't have time to do all her work, let alone take time out to talk to a life coach. But the thought kept niggling at her, especially when coaching seemed to be all over the TV and in the magazines she read.

A few times, she'd meant to find out more about coaching, but something always seemed to get in the way and she never got round to it. Once, she even went online to see which coaches were available in her area, but she was too tired to do anything more than look.

Sarah decided to take a couple of weeks' holiday with her fiancé and took a book on personal development with her to read on the beach. With time to reflect, she began to understand what her friends had been telling her, but she'd been too busy and stressed to think about – she had been swept along by her job and lost her sense of herself.

The book was great and motivated her to do something about it, but she knew that when she got back to work, she wouldn't get round to it on her own. She made a decision that when she got back, she'd find herself a life coach. She had some money set aside and, with her fiancé, agreed that it would be worth the investment. When she arrived back home, she unpacked her bag and at 10pm, she fired up the computer to look at the websites of coaches in her area – she found them through a search engine.

The first coach looked good, but didn't show his prices on the site. Judging from the types of people he said he coached – high-powered company directors and business owners, Sarah assumed that he was probably too expensive, so she carried on looking.

The second coach seemed to coach people like her and the prices were affordable. She looked around, but she couldn't find a phone number or e-mail address. Finally she clicked on a tab that took her to a form where she was asked to fill in her details. She did so, even answering some quite personal questions, but she wasn't clear about what would happen next.

The third coach surprised her by talking to her from the website! From the sound of her voice, she seemed like someone Sarah could open up to and the coach's photo looked nice – a woman a few years older than her with a pleasant, approachable smile. On that page were comments from people who Annie (the coach) had worked with and she could click through to read articles about Annie in the press. Her prices were a little higher than the other coach, but she felt a connection with Annie – plus she was good enough to be featured in a lifestyle magazine – so Sarah decided to send an e-mail to the address on her site asking whether Annie could give her a call to explain more about coaching. Straight away, Sarah received a reply from Annie – at 10.30pm! – telling her that she'd give her a call back the following day.

The next day Annie picked up her e-mails, saw the message from Sarah and called her straight away. (The 'reply' Sarah had received the night before was from Annie's autoresponder.) They got on well on the phone and Sarah booked a package of sessions, with the first appointment that week. What made it even easier for her was that she could pay online using her 0% credit card and then spread out the repayments.

Incidentally, Sarah never heard back from the other coach, which disappointed her, but she was so happy with Annie that she didn't worry too much about it – their loss.

It's sometimes easy to forget that clients could have been building up to working with a coach for a long time. When they do decide to find a coach, they often want to start as quickly as possible. Whilst people rarely wake up one morning and think, *"Hmm... what shall I do today? I know I'll get a life coach"*, many do wake up and say *"I've put it off too long already – today's the day I'll find a life coach."*

And when they do get in touch with you (whether they've found you online or through another marketing method such as networking) they expect to be able to speak to you and make a decision as quickly as possible. They've waited long enough already – don't keep them hanging on!

I'm often astonished by the numbers of examples I hear of people contacting coaches by e-mail or by leaving messages on their voice-mail and never hearing back from them. I'd be surprised if there are many coaches who can afford to turn down business from clients who are eager to hire them. Simply by getting in touch with people within 24 hours of their enquiry can put you ahead of other coaches and allow you to start building rapport with them before the other coaches have even spoken to them.

In the example earlier, Annie had started to build rapport with Sarah without even knowing it – Sarah knew what she looked like, how she sounded and even had an e-mail from Annie before Annie was aware that Sarah had been on her site.

What do you say?

Forget trying to 'sell' coaching or even 'selling yourself'. Clients who call you want to talk about one thing and one thing only – themselves. So before you launch into your pitch, ask questions. Find out:

- Background – what has led them to this point?
- How much they know about coaching
- Whether they have been coached before
- What they'd like to achieve through coaching
- What are their reasons for thinking that coaching is the right approach for them?
- What they are looking for in a coach

Allow yourself **at least** 15 minutes to speak to a prospective client on the phone. As you find out more information, you'll get a sense of what they're like as a person and whether you want to work with them.

Some people don't really know what to expect when they call a coach for the first time and don't know what they should be asking you. Whilst the client is telling you about their background and what they want to achieve, you can start to build rapport, trust and credibility by talking about whether you can identify with what they're saying, reassure them that they're not alone and you have successfully coached people in similar situations, e.g. *"I coached someone who was going through something similar and they found that..."* Don't dominate the conversation, though. As a general guide, they should be doing about 60-80% of the talking, with you doing 20-40%. At this stage, concentrate on *relationship building*.

If someone asks you what you think they should do, gently explain that coaching is not advice and *when they book a coaching session*, you will help them to find their own solution. This initial conversation is for both of you to find out more about whether you would work well together – it is not a coaching session. Even if you're offering a free taster session, you should have a preliminary conversation with them first so that they are well-informed about coaching and they get the most from the taster. You want them to come back, don't you?!

Throughout the conversation, keep your tone light, approachable and SMILE when you're talking to them. Believe me – you can hear when someone's smiling and when they're not.

It's only once you've got the background information and found out what they want to achieve that you should start to discuss the types of coaching on offer, whether you coach face-to-face, how your packages work and how much your rates are.

Be clear in your mind about what you offer and how your packages are structured. It can help to stick or pin up a sheet of paper next to your phone that states your rates and how you work – just in case your mind goes blank. Sometimes it does – especially if someone's asking what your prices are when they are either including or excluding VAT and what you'd charge for 3, 6, 12 or 24 sessions or any other package you might not have considered before.

Be proud of your rates and when stating them, be bold. Practice talking about your rates with a friend until you are completely comfortable discussing them. To avoid *that* pause after you've given your rates, simply continue speaking and explain what's included in the price.

For example:

Them: *"How much do you charge for coaching?"*

You: *"I charge £250 per month and that includes three hour-long coaching sessions on the phone, plus unlimited e-mail support and emergency 10 minute 'laser coaching' sessions if you need them. What's good about that is that if you're about to go into an important meeting and you want to think through how you're going to handle the situation we can speak about it first. As you're a business person and you told me you'd like to be more confident in meetings, I imagine that that would be quite useful, wouldn't it?"*

Them: *"Yes, it would, I didn't realize that coaching could work like that..."*

The price is a *feature* of what you offer. People buy *benefits*. The *benefit* of signing up for a monthly package is that they will get coaching that is flexible enough to help them to achieve their goals.

Compare this to a conversation where you stated the price and stopped talking:

Them: *"How much do you charge for coaching?"*

You: *"£75 per hour."*

Them: *"How much?! That seems very expensive."*

Price perceptions

In relative terms, coaching *can* seem expensive. It's probably more than they would pay for a massage or a treatment at a back specialist...but hang on a minute, coaching has the power to change a person's life!

If you can help your client to achieve their goals, what's that actually worth to them? What is it worth to:

- Get a promotion and a £5,000 pay rise?
- Save an ailing marriage?
- Stand up to a workplace bully?
- Find a new career they love?
- Have more family time with their children?

The *results* they got from coaching will be remembered long after they've forgotten how much they paid for it.

Sometimes clients will tell you that your rates are much higher than they expected to pay. Before panicking and dropping your rates, do some investigation to find out what they expected to pay and what they based their expectation on. Usually when you ask clients how much they expected to pay, they'll tell you, *"Well, I'm not sure really, I've never done this before and it seems like a lot of money."*

At this point you can assure them that your rate *is* in line with coaches of similar levels of experience and expertise, and yes, if they look hard they will be able to find cheaper coaches out there. But is cheaper necessarily better? We're talking about their life here! Remind them how you differentiate yourself from other coaches – you have got proof that you get results, you are a recognized expert as you have a book/speak at events, etc.

Provided you know your prices are in line with the market rate for your experience and *what the market's prepared to pay*, stick to your guns.

This is where understanding your market is very important.

A coach with ten years' proven coaching experience and thousands of coaching hours under their belt may very easily be getting hourly rates of £500 or more from large corporate companies, but if they decide to coach individuals, they will have to accept that few individuals will be prepared to pay the same amount (unless they are very wealthy). Even with all their impressive coaching experience, a middle manager coming to them for career coaching may struggle to pay them £150 per hour and say they're too expensive. The client would be comparing them with other coaches who are charging less, because that is the amount the *market is prepared to pay*.

"I'd just like to have one session for now...."

Depending on the type of coaching you do, it may be appropriate to offer one-off sessions. Some examples might be coaching on:

- Interview techniques
- Preparation for a difficult meeting
- Making an important decision

But, if coaching is to help the client to make long-term changes, in almost all cases, they need more than one session to do it. The majority of clients need to work with a coach for at least three months for them to change underlying behaviours and thinking patterns. Techniques such as NLP (Neuro-Linguistic Programming) and TFT (Thought Field Therapy) can help to accelerate their personal development, but in order to support your client through making their own personal changes and helping them to deal with how other people react to them changing takes a few months. Of course, how many sessions a client has within those three months is up to them. Plus, realistically how much can you cover in just one session? The first session, or 'intake session', usually takes longer than an ordinary session because you've got to go through the background and help them to set goals for the coaching programme. Will your client get the benefits they want from one session alone?

Find out from the client *why* they only want to commit to one session.

If they are on a limited budget and won't be able to afford more coaching, working with a coach may not be the best solution for them *right now*. Your job as a coach is not to put people in a position where they have to make a decision between paying you and missing a payment on their mortgage. Your job is to get the best result for the client and right now, their money might be better spent on a self-help book. Suggest a few good books to them and put them on your newsletter list so that they can get tips and articles that might help them. When they're in a position to be able to afford coaching, they'll be back.

If there are other reasons such as they're not sure how coaching works or whether they'll 'click' with you, find out what they need to know to put their minds at rest. Would it be helpful if you explained how a session usually works? Could you tell them about a recent success story and send them some testimonials from recent clients? If they're local, could you meet face-to-face for an informal chat?

Not all coaches are prepared to do one-off sessions and if you're not, tell the client so and be ready to explain why.

What if they're not my type of client?

Of course, there will be some people who contact you who are not the types of clients you want to work with, but they might just be perfect for another coach you know.

If someone is on a budget and can't afford to pay much for coaching, you can refer them to another coach who's trying to break into their area and needs experience or a coach in the *pre-launch* stage of their business. If someone wants a particular type of coaching that you don't feel comfortable doing you could refer them to someone else and know that one day they'll do the same for you.

Even if there are clients that coaching isn't appropriate for, you can build networks of counsellors, therapists, consultants, etc who you can refer people to and they can do the same for you.

However, if you've got targeted marketing, this shouldn't be a problem for you as prospective clients will know about you and the type of people you work with, before they call. Your website and other marketing materials will screen out the clients who aren't a good match for you.

Getting commitment

You've had a nice chat, found out more about them and they know the rates. How do you move it on?

Ask for the business!

You can do this by asking, *"So, would you like to go ahead? I've got a couple of appointments available next week. How does 10am on Tuesday or 4pm on Wednesday suit you?"*

When they say yes and choose an appointment, book them in and explain exactly what happens next:

- You'll be sending them a coaching a*greement* (the word 'contract' can sound a bit formal) to fill in and return
- How the coaching session will happen – where you'll meet or when they have to call you (make sure *they* realize that they call *you*, not the other way around)
- You'll send them an invoice
- When they need to pay
- How they can pay – do you have options on this?
- Your *postponement* policy (not cancellation)

Some people will need you to explain things to them in minute details, others will be more laid back. Either way, for your own piece of mind, make sure you cover everything up front so there's no room for misunderstandings – especially over the postponement policy. Talk in terms of 'moving' a session, rather than 'cancelling' a session – otherwise by mentioning it you might make them think that it's usual for people to cancel and you don't want that!

Getting the phone to ring in the first place

"Great", you might say. *"That's fine if you've got people calling you – what do you do if no one's calling?"*

Be proactive! Do you have details of people who have contacted you in the past and went away to 'think about it' and you never heard from them? Pick up the phone and find out how they're getting on. Equally, contact past clients who you haven't been in touch with for three months or more and find out how they're doing – you never know, they might be interested in having a refresher or 'top-up' session. This includes people who you did pro bono or free coaching with – just remember to tell them you're a fully-fledged coach and you have a commercial practice now, i.e. you'll be charging! You could offer them a special rate as a past client.

Go through the lists of people who have attended your seminars and workshops to do a follow-up with them. Ask whether they enjoyed the talk and you're calling to find out whether they would like any one-to-one help to apply some of the things they learned in the workshop. In conversation, explain how you've helped other people and tell them some recent success stories.

Get out your business card box and catch up with people you've met networking. Ask them more about what they do and find out whether they'd be interested in meeting for a coffee to find out more about one another's businesses. At the meeting, explain how you work and ask if it's something they'd be interested in. Also ask about who they know who might be keen on having an exploratory (no obligation) conversation about coaching. Tell them what to listen out for that would indicate that someone might benefit from coaching, e.g. *"I'm working such long hours"* or *"I'm having trouble with my staff."*

Go through the details of people who have responded to your other marketing initiatives or who are on your newsletter subscription list. Call a few at random.

Finally, give people a reason to take action now – not next month or when they feel like it – **now**. You could offer 7 sessions for the price of 6 when you book before the end of the month. You could offer a free upgrade to the next package, e.g. get a Platinum package for the price of a Gold package. You might give away a free book or CD to people who book this week. Or you could joint venture with someone and offer a free session with, say, an image consultant when you book a six month coaching programme.

Give people a call to action when you speak to them in the same way that you would when doing your marketing in any other format.

Section 2 Organizations

Many of the tips in Section 1 apply to closing the deal in the business or organizational environment, but the process can take much longer.

Typical lead times from first speaking to a contact at an organization to starting working with them range from 6 months to 18 months.

The reason for this is that the decision usually has to be approved by several people in the organization. The lead time is usually shorter when dealing with the owner of a small SME (Small to Medium-sized Enterprise) than it is for a large hierarchical organization.

There are lots of factors to consider:

- Are they currently using a coach or coaches?
- If they are, are they happy with them?
- If they are not using coaches do they plan to?
- What budget do they have available?
- Can they afford you?
- Are you speaking to the decision-maker?
- Are you a good match for what they're looking for in a coach?
- Do they even know what they want in a coach?
- How sceptical are they about coaching?
- Are their competitors/peers working with coaches?

Because the processes are slightly different for different sizes of organizations, let's talk about them separately.

Sole traders (one person working alone)

The way that you 'close' for a sole trader is very similar to dealing with individuals because even though the business may be paying for coaching *on paper*, in reality the money's coming out of their own pockets.

When talking to sole traders about coaching, you need to be able to demonstrate that they will get tangible benefits from it. Being vague about coaching won't help your case. Think about it from their perspective and understand what the benefits to them might be. They are very unlikely to have included a budget for coaching in their business plan – they need to be sure it's worth the money.

Depending on your niche, you may need to work hard to demonstrate a track-record in helping people like them – this could be that you've coached people like them before, you were a consultant advising people like them or you have run your own business before. They may want to know who they can speak to who will vouch for you.

Remember: Experience, credibility and contacts get you clients.

Small businesses (approx 2-50 people)

The buying decision is probably not made by one person alone. Depending on the size and type of organization, decisions may have to go to a committee – this is particularly the case with partnerships and family-owned businesses. Whilst you may be dealing with the Managing Director, who is a shareholder in the business, they may need approval from the Board to invest money in their own or someone else's personal development.

It is important to find out as early as possible whether they have the authority to make a decision on whether to go ahead and spend money on coaching. Because of this, you could have to have several phone calls and/or meetings before you find out for definite if they will be hiring you. Try wherever possible to meet everyone who is involved in the decision.

Businesses usually plan and manage their cashflow on a monthly basis, so you are likely to have more success presenting a proposal for coaching on a fixed monthly fee, rather than charging by the hour. It also makes things easier from your point of view because you know how much to invoice for each month.

As with sole traders, you need to demonstrate that they will get measurable results from coaching. Someone, somewhere in the business will be asked to explain exactly what they got for their money further down the track. Unfortunately, business owners don't like to part with their profits just to get a nice warm fuzzy feeling inside. This may be their first experience of hiring a coach, so be sure that you give them enough information to feel that they are making a good business decision and their most important assets – their people – are in good hands.

Medium-sized enterprises (approx 50-250 people)

Organizations of this size will usually have some budget allocated to Training and Development, sometimes called Learning and Development, that will be managed by a specific person. This may be a full-time job for them or they may be one of the Directors or Partners who takes responsibility for the development of their people.

If you're going in cold, i.e. you haven't been recommended by someone, be aware that organizations of this size are approached by coaches, consultants and trainers on a regular basis, and they may already have people who they're using.

Do your homework and find out as much as possible about them, their culture and what they're interested in before making an appointment to meet with the decision maker.

They will have experience of meeting with other people like you, so whilst it's good for them to understand your personal philosophy on coaching, don't spend an hour 'selling' *coaching*. The chances are they know what it is because someone's already been in a few weeks or months before and told them.

If you have the opportunity to meet a decision-maker, make sure they understand how you're different from other coaches. Emphasize your background and how your experience is relevant to them. I know that as coaches we don't need to have walked in the clients' shoes to coach effectively, but *they* need to know that they won't have to spend their entire session explaining how their role fits into the organizational structure or teaching you industry jargon. They will want you to hit the ground running and coach – not pay you to learn about something they'd expect you to know anyway.

Large organizations (250+ people)

Everything that applied for small and medium-sized organizations applies here, but crank up the professionalism!

There's a high probability that a number of people in the organization have been coached before or are currently being coached. When you get the opportunity to have a meeting, you are likely to be interviewed to, if you're successful, become part of a panel of coaches they use.

Prepare for the meeting in the same way you would for a job interview. Go to their website and read about their history, culture and how they develop their people. Search the internet to find stories about them, particularly any references to people joining, leaving or being recognized with awards. Find out from your network of contacts if anyone they know does or used to work there, and what it's like on the inside. Find out what people usually wear to work – what is appropriate for their culture? Prepare!

You will be judged on your coaching experience, your style of coaching and the types of people you coach. You must cover this in the meeting. They need to know this to understand who within the organization they could match up with you. It's also helpful for them to understand how many people you've coached in their particular field as it demonstrates experience and credibility.

Perhaps most important of all is whether you're their kind of person. Remember when you worked out what you stand for and how you want to be perceived? This is show time!

Let's say your research tells you that the organization is very traditional in its approach and everyone wears a suit. This could be a problem if you are, and want to be perceived as, laid-back. What a dilemma! A more laid-back approach might be just what they need or it could scare them off. The trouble is, until you have the meeting, you won't know what they want. Or will you?

Scan their website again and look for their mission statement or any other statements that give you a clue to *their* brand values. Look at the photos on their site, particularly the photos of their directors, to give you clues as to how *they* want to be perceived. This isn't foolproof, but it will give you something to work with. If in doubt, dress smart and get ready to use your rapport building skills when you're in the meeting.

You can adjust the way you come across when you're eyeball to eyeball with the person you're meeting.

When you leave the meeting you should be clear about what happens next – are they actively looking for a coach or are your details going to be filed away ready to be pulled out when someone needs a coach? Be sure that you understand what's going to happen next.

Negotiating your terms

With organizations you may be asked to coach more than one person or even a whole team. When you're discussing terms with them, aim for a fixed half day or day rate when you come to their office and coach several people, rather than coming in for an hour here and an hour there. It is more cost effective for both you and the client.

Also find out whether the organization operates a purchase order system – this means that they need to give you a purchase order number to quote on your invoice to ensure that your invoice is paid. Some organizations won't pay invoices without quoting this number. It's not unheard of for organizations to stall paying invoices for months because there's no purchase order number and then when you do finally get one, they won't pay it until next month, because you've missed this month's payment run!

Be clear about the terms you're agreeing with your client:

- How much you're charging
- Whether you will be paid in advance or not
- Whether you need to quote a purchase order number
- How quickly your invoices will be paid
- Whether you can claim for travel expenses

It's good to confirm this in a letter to your contact at the organization so that you have it in writing. Some smaller businesses will be happy to sign your usual coaching agreement form, but larger organizations can be reluctant to sign anything that looks like a contract. A confirmation letter stating the agreed terms and what you've agreed with them – frequency of sessions, postponement policy, etc – should be sufficient.

Summary

- Individual prospective clients and organizations need to be approached in different ways when it comes to asking for the business
- Individuals could have been thinking about getting a coach for months before they contact you – when they do, they expect you to respond quickly
- If you fail to contact prospective clients within 24 of their enquiry, you could miss out
- When you first speak to people about coaching, focus on asking questions, not selling
- Be clear about your pricing structure and what's included in your packages
- Get the client to think about what coaching is worth, not how much it costs
- When people ask for one-off sessions, find out more about their reasons behind it
- Be proactive and call people back
- Sole traders are paying for coaching out of their own pockets and need reassurance
- When approaching small businesses remember that someone else may be involved in the buying decision
- In meetings with medium and large organizations don't waste time on 'selling' coaching generically, tell them about your experience and capabilities
- Get your terms in writing and be clear about how you will be paid

chapter twelve Creating Your Marketing Plan

TWELVE Creating Your Marketing Plan

A marketing plan is simply a written statement of your marketing goals and how you intend to achieve them. This chapter takes you through each of the different marketing methods and helps you to decide when to use them to promote your practice.

Depending on which phase your practice is in – *pre-launch, launch* or *maturity* – you may decide to have slightly different messages with different outcomes. For example:

Coaching practice in pre-launch phase

Desired outcome:	Get experience and build confidence
SMART goal:	In six months time I will have coached 10 people for at least 4 sessions each
Message:	Free life coaching sessions

Coaching practice in launch phase

Desired outcome:	Start charging for coaching sessions and be able to switch to being employed full-time to part-time
SMART goal:	In two months time I will have at least three regular clients each paying me £175 per month
Message:	Stress coaching for care workers

Coaching practice in maturity phase

Desired outcome:	Move from personal coaching into executive coaching
SMART goal:	In six months time I will be regularly coaching five School Heads on leadership and management at £500 per month each. This will represent 50% of my income from coaching, with the remainder from personal coaching clients.
Message:	Improve staff retention and motivation levels

EXERCISE

Write down the goals for your own coaching practice. What do you want things to be like in the next:

6 months:

12 months:

2 years:

Is your market seasonal?

The demand for some types of coaching is seasonal, the challenge is to identify when people are most likely to want to have coaching. For example, if you are targeting middle managers hoping for promotion, the number of people considering career coaching usually peaks when they have time off work to relax and 'take stock'. This would mean increasing your marketing to coincide with holiday periods such as summer or Christmas.

Key problems and challenges

Just as demand for coaching can be seasonal, the issues your clients want to be coached on can change according to the time of year. For example, accountants experience more stress at the end of the tax year than at any other time. You should time when your marketing messages appear, for example in your newsletters and PR, so that they are relevant message and have a call to action.

Planning ahead

Over the next few pages, we will be going through the main marketing methods to examine how far in advance you need to start planning to make sure your marketing messages appear at the right time.

Networking

Networking is one of the fastest ways to get your message out in the world. There are networking events happening on a daily basis, the trick is to find the ones that give you the greatest chance of accessing your target clients. It's worth investing some time to visit the websites of the local groups and events to plan which events you'd like to go to.

When you've found the right places to network, it can take time to build up good working relationships with them to the point where they are prepared to recommend you to their business contacts and friends. With a targeted approach, you can start having follow-up meetings with people almost immediately.

With a bit of luck and keeping your ears and eyes open to opportunities, you can find that your networks will bring you good results, but you do still need to give people time to trust you. Remember, it's better to build solid relationships with a smaller group of people that flitting around and not getting to know anyone beyond a very superficial level.

EXERCISE

Visit the websites of the groups that can connect you with your target clients. Make a note of four events that you can attend in the next two months and make a commitment to go!

Public Relations (PR)/publicity

Timing is crucial with PR and depends on whether you are submitting ideas for a feature or a news story. Below are very rough guidelines on when you should first get in touch with the journalist to pitch the idea. The dates are given are in advance of publication date (refer back to Advertising section for more info). You should always try to get hold of a 'Forward Features' list from their advertising department to help you to plan ahead. Then call the journalist to find out when they will be researching for that feature.

	Features	News Stories
Weekly local newspaper	1 month	1 week
Daily newspaper	3-6 months	2 days
Local monthly magazines	3-6 month	3-4 weeks
National monthly magazines	4-5 months	2-3 months
Radio	6 months	2-3 days
TV	6-12 months	2-3 days

EXERCISE

Write down all the types of PR and Publicity that you would like to get and when you need to start planning for them. Call a couple of publications and ask for a 'Forward Features' list.

Public speaking

Event organizers tend to plan who they are going to ask to speak about 4-6 months ahead. With some events such as conferences and exhibitions where there will be a printed show guide, speakers will be booked even further in advance.

To maximize your exposure in *their* marketing to support the event, aim to contact organizers at least 6 months in advance of when you'd like to appear as there may be an interview process you need to go through or they may want to come and see you speak somewhere else first.

Once the event organizers have used you as a speaker, the lead time shortens considerably. It has been known for organizers to call speakers the day before an event because another speaker has let them down! You can be prepared for this by having a couple of talks that you deliver regularly so that you don't have to spend days preparing for it.

EXERCISE

Write a list of the places where you'd like to speak and when you would most like to do it. Write down the topic you'd like to speak on, particularly if it is a seasonal topic, and some bullet points of what you'd like to cover in the talk. Plan when you will speak to the organizers.

Internet

Timings for producing a good quality website vary enormously and will depend on how complex you want your site to be. You should speak to your website designer about this. Also think about whether you want to launch your website in phases, e.g. start with a simple one-page site, then add other pages later.

EXERCISE

Write down all the stages that you'll need to go through to construct your website and how long you expect them to take. Remember to include planning the pages, writing the content, setting up the technical aspects such as registering domain names and organizing hosting. When do you want your website to go live?

Advertising

Below are typical booking deadlines (when you need to book the space/airtime) and copy deadlines (the last date that you can supply them with your advert). The dates given are a **rough guide** to the numbers of days, weeks or months in advance of the publication date. You should always check the exact dates with the publication. The publication date is the date that the magazine, newspaper, etc is on sale/distributed. This should not be confused with the date on the cover of the magazine, for example the June issue of Marie Claire actually comes out in May.

	Booking deadline	**Copy Deadline**
Weekly local newspaper	2-3 weeks	1 week
Daily newspaper	3-4 days	2 days
Local monthly magazines	1 month	2 weeks
National monthly magazines	2 months	1 month
Radio	2 months	2 weeks

These dates do not allow for the time you need to get your advert ready, e.g. briefing graphic designer, making amendments, writing and recording radio adverts. You should speak to your designer or marketing consultant about this.

EXERCISES

1. Find out lead times for all the advertising methods that you plan to use to promote your practice.
2. Find out how long it would take a graphic designer to produce an advertisement for you.

Direct marketing, sales letters, postcards

If you are printing your own letters, you should allow enough time to get the database of names and addresses ready, write the letter, print them off, stuff envelopes and put them in the post.

If you're getting postcards printed by a local printer, you should get lead times from them. They will usually turn a small job around in approximately 3-4 days from receiving your finished artwork. But you must call them at least a week in advance so that they can book your print job in. Then you should allow time to address the postcards and mail them out.

EXERCISE

Write down how long you expect it to take for you to produce your mailer. Remember to allow time for you to buy in a mailing list (if necessary), brief a graphic designer (if you're sending a postcard), brief a copywriter (if you decide to get someone else to write your letter for you) and get the relevant stationery (letterhead, envelopes, stamps and any 'stuffers' that you want to include in the envelope, e.g. press cuttings).

Flyers, brochures, stationery

Timings for flyers and brochures depend very much on what you are producing. If you are designing and printing your own flyers, these can be produced within a matter of hours, but if you are producing a glossy brochure, you may need to allow 6 weeks when starting from scratch. Remember to include time for briefing your designer and making amendments where necessary.

EXERCISE

Write down how long you expect it to take to produce your flyers, brochures or stationery.

Newsletters

Timings vary enormously depending on whether you are sending your newsletter out by e-mail or by post. It also depends on whether you are writing your newsletter yourself or if you are briefing a copywriter to do it for you. If you are writing your own newsletter and sending it out by e-mail, give yourself a couple of days to write, check and format your newsletter. If you are getting someone else to write it for you and you'll be sending your newsletters by mail, allow yourself 3-4 weeks from writing the brief to when the newsletters will arrive.

EXERCISE

Write down how long you expect it to take to write and distribute your newsletters.

Delegation

The secret of all good business owners, entrepreneurs and successful coaches is that they know their limitations. This is VERY different from having limiting beliefs!

Knowing your limitations is being realistic about when you're the best person to do a particular job and when to hand it over to someone who's either more experienced, or more capable of doing it right first time. It is also understanding when your time would be better spent doing something else.

For example, is it a good use of your time to design all your own stationery? If you have got a background in design, you're confident that you will do a good job and you enjoy it, by all means you can do it yourself. But if it's going to take you two solid weeks to get it done right and you will have pulled your hair out in the process whilst achieving nothing else in that time, it is a waste of time. Time to call in an expert!

EXERCISES

1. List everything that you'll need to do in your practice, including all the elements of your marketing that you've identified so far. Include EVERYTHING from opening the post and sending out invoices to booking sales appointments with prospective business clients and networking, and don't forget time spent actually *coaching your clients*! Then add in the things that if you had more time, you would do such as writing a book, attending seminars, checking in with past clients and asking them for referrals.
2. Now go down the list and mark the things that you absolutely **have** to do yourself. These are the things that no one else in the world could do, even if you owned a large multinational corporation with thousands of staff. Then look at the list again and see if there are tasks that you could group together and delegate, e.g. sending invoices and chasing payments, cold calling and sending out brochures.

EXERCISES (CONTINUED)

3. Then ask yourself who *could* do these things for you. For example, you could use a freelancer to write and send out press releases, someone else to attend meetings with you and write minutes, a telemarketing company to call your database of clients to book sales appointments, a virtual receptionist to answer your phones when you are not there or you are busy coaching a client. The beauty of doing this is that it's pay-as-you-go. You don't pay for staff to sit around twiddling their thumbs when they are not needed.
4. The next step is to think about any tasks that could be automated, such as sending newsletters or promotional announcements to your clients or prospective clients by e-mail. Also, booking coaching sessions, downloading your brochure online and/or reminding you to call someone a couple of days after you've met them at a networking event.

Writing a brief for your supplier

Once you've identified areas of your marketing where you can get some help, you can save yourself a lot of time, money and lost sleep by writing an effective brief for your supplier.

A brief helps your supplier to understand exactly what you want, what you want it to achieve and when you want to get it back from them. If you don't start off with a clear brief, it will take much longer for your suppliers to get it right, especially if you're not really sure what you're after. For example, you could expect a very expensive bill if you turn up to see a website designer and say, *"I want to have a website, but I'm not sure what I want it to look like, what I want it to include or what I want it to do."*

Writing the brief also helps you to get very clear about what you're doing and why.

EXERCISE

Choose one of the marketing activities that you can outsource and fill in the brief below. If you need to change or add sections, feel free to do so.

Title of project
Date of brief
Brief description of project
What is the marketing message you want to get across?
Objective – What do you want the person seeing or hearing this marketing message to think, feel, do, etc?
Target audience, i.e. who are you talking to?
What are the main problems / challenges facing them and how can you help?
Why should they use you?
Are you running any special offers or other incentives for them to get in touch now?
What tone of voice should be used, e.g. serious, humourous, casual?

What text would you like to include in this project?
Are there any photos or logos you want to include?
What *exactly* do you want the finished project to be like? How many words do you want in the press release? How many pages on the website? How big will the advert be? Etc.
Deadline for first draft, i.e. when should they send it back to you for comments?
Deadline for final sign-off, i.e. when the project has to be completely finished, for example, when you need to send the artwork to the printer
Other notes

Setting your marketing budget

Your marketing budget is simply money that you have set aside for marketing your coaching practice. You should allocate a certain amount each month for your marketing and try not to spend more than that.

It can be very easy to spend all of your marketing budget in one go. You need to concentrate your budget on marketing that is likely to get you clients, both in the short-term and the long-term. Bear in mind that some of the marketing activities you invest your budget in may not give you immediate results, but you need to keep on doing them to get clients in the long-term, for example a newsletter is a very good way of building rapport with prospective clients, but it may take some of them 6-12 months to become paying clients.

Of course, there will be certain things that you need to invest in up-front when you start, but try to spread your budget out so that you have money available to take advantage of special offers or unexpected marketing activities.

The simplest way of working out your marketing budget is to find out how much each of your chosen marketing activities will cost. Base your budget on the full price, but negotiate hard when you come to actually booking!

Top tip: You may be able to barter to get some of the services you need free of charge. For example, would your graphic designer be interested in receiving coaching to the value of the work that he/she does for you?

EXERCISE

Find out how much each of your marketing activities is likely to cost. You can use an estimate if you're not sure exactly how much it will be.

Summary

- Set your goals based on the phase that your coaching practice is in – pre-launch, launch or maturity
- If your market is seasonal, plan when in the year your messages need to appear
- Networking is one of the fastest marketing methods as there are events and group meetings daily
- Planning for PR can take weeks or months depending on the medium you want to be featured in
- Setting up a website can take longer than you think – get advice from your designer before committing to a 'live' date
- Advertising can be placed fairly quickly, but you need to allow time to get the advertisement itself ready
- Direct mail can be very fast, but has a number of things that you need to do and, like getting a website designed, can take longer than you think
- Flyers, brochures and stationery can usually be produced from start to finish in 6 weeks or less
- The time you take to produce a newsletter depends on whether you are writing the content yourself and how you intend to distribute the newsletter

- You don't have to do everything yourself. There are some tasks that are better delegated to other people to allow you to concentrate on what you are good at
- Make a decision on how much you are prepared to spend on your marketing
- You may be able to barter for services

chapter thirteen Making It Happen!

THIRTEEN Making It Happen!

In this book you have been given the secrets to starting and building a coaching practice. You can be assured that everything you have read here has been tried, tested and is the product of years of blood, sweat and tears.

What you choose to do with the knowledge you now have is up to you. You can choose to:

- Ignore it and carry on as you are
- Tell yourself that you will do something about it...one day
- Make excuses about why it wouldn't work for you

Or, you could:

- Take the initiative and try something new

Your destiny is in your hands. You alone have the power to make yourself a success but you have to be prepared to take the rough with the smooth and have the courage to push yourself forward – even on the days when you don't seem to be making any progress.

Make a promise to yourself that every day you'll do something – no matter how tiny – that helps you to get your message out there in the world. It could be something small like putting a marketing message in your e-mail signature or something bold and outrageous like phoning up your local radio station to ask for a regular slot! It really doesn't matter what it is, just take action and do *something*! And do it consistently – remember, 7 contacts!

You CAN do it!

The Coach Files

The Coach Files

In the next section you can read frank interviews with people who have become known for niche marketing their coaching services.

As you read through their interviews, you'll discover how they got started and some of the lessons they learned along the way.

COACH FILE

Name: Guy Levine

Niche: Internet Marketing

Website: www.guylevine.com

How did you choose your niche?

I think that my niche really chose me. I started out designing websites for people and building some .com ideas. After having a big win in the .com arena, lots of people started asking me to help them with their websites and internet marketing strategy. I suppose my niche came about because it was the only thing I knew how to do. I did not take it tight to a group of people for a long time.

Did you have a niche right from the start?

No, I was more interested in making some money. I realized that the key to successful marketing in the beginning is building up momentum – working with as many different people as possible and starting to earn some money. Then I started to focus more on the people I liked working with and the 'profitable' target markets.

When did you realize that having a niche would help you to market yourself?

I was lucky as once I found people I liked working with, they would shout about me to their friends. I then realized that I didn't just need to find a niche, but also a 'big shot' within that niche to sing my praises. Once you have that, life is much easier.

How long did it take for you to establish yourself as 'the' coach for that niche?

Probably about 1-2 years. I am quite 'in your face' and not scared to shout about myself. This really helped. So many people I know are the worlds best kept secrets. Don't ever be afraid to self-promote!

What have you learned most about marketing yourself as a coach?

Always sell an end result. People didn't ever want coaching from me, they wanted more people to visit their website, or more customers from the website. How I did it was not important to them. I also realized I could charge more for an outcome as it was more tangible. I always liken it to a craftsman building a table, he doesn't say I'm going to hammer and saw and chisel, he says I'm going to build a table. How he builds it is not my problem!

How much of a difference did it make when you could promote yourself as a published writer/speaker as well as a coach?

Speaking is my main marketing tool. I love doing it, and am right up there with the best speakers. I regularly work abroad and get well paid. It does help, but for me, it's being able to speak to lots of people at the same time instead of having to work a room. Having international speaking gigs on your bio also helps with credibility.

Did you make any mistakes when you were setting up? Were there any howlers??

No mistakes, only tests that proved they were wrong. Apple green business cards, forgetting to take business cards, saying some really stupid things on stage, not looking smart enough (clothes), taking customer service for granted. Oh yes, and walking into the ladies toilet by mistake before a large talk and bumping into one of the delegates!

What's your key to success?

Constant movement. Never give up, or be defeated by others. There are so many people who are not even that good at coaching who make loads of money. If they can do it, so can you. I also like to self promote as much as possible. No one else will shout about you so you have to get on and do it. I remember once reading 'I'm tired of waiting for success so I'll just start without it.'

What advice would you give to new coaches who want a wide range of clients and don't want to be 'pigeon-holed' as a certain type of coach/the coach for a certain type of client?

The best source for new clients is the people you know and the people they know. They will be free to market to. Give them a 'no brainer' that they can't refuse, but don't be afraid to charge.

What is your ideal client like?

My ideal client is someone who wants to start marketing their business via the internet and other powerful marketing methods. So many people get their marketing wrong. They market like they still live in the middle ages. Marketing is simple, give people a solution to a problem they have. I help people find and package the solution, and then tell as many people as possible about it.

COACH FILE

Name: Chris Barrow

Niche: Dentists

Website: www.thedentalbusinessschool.com

How did you choose your niche?

I didn't – it chose me. From 1994 to 1997 I was transitioning from full-time financial planner to full-time coach – my marketing was done by public speaking and I would travel anywhere, anytime to get a 'gig' – it's all about visibility. My definition of a client was any small professional service firm owner who would pay me. There were few rules and no niche. In 1996 I started, through word of mouth recommendation, to get invitations to speak at dental conferences. One thing led to another and I noticed the demand and enquired as to the reason – which was a lot of pain in the market around survival in the post-NHS world (its still going on!). By mid-1997 I saw the niche and went for it full-time in 1998. I've been there ever since.

When did you realize that having a niche would help you to market yourself?

When the repeat requests started coming in for 'gigs' and I realized that dentists are what Dan Sullivan calls 'ideal clients' – slow learners with deep pockets.

How long did it take for you to establish yourself as 'the' coach for that niche?

I would say that it was three years of 'gigging' and submitting articles before I began to be recognized by a significant number of the profession – I'm now in my 9th year in the niche and recently voted as the 30th most influential person in UK dentistry (one of only three non dentists in the list and the other two are national politicians).

What have you learned most about marketing yourself as a coach?

That visibility is the key – I speak, I write and I'm still doing both as actively now as I was 9 years ago. The market constantly needs reminding that you exist and that you are useful to know.

How much of a difference did it make when you could promote yourself as a published writer/speaker as well as a coach?

I co-authored 'Profitable Dental Practice' and published about three years ago. It's a highly specialized and small market, so we have only sold about 1000 copies but it has considerably enhanced my credibility and reputation. No doubt about it. By the way, the co-author was a well-published Professor of Dentistry at a highly-regarded dental school – that helped, of course. I contributed 80% content and 20% writing – he contributed 80% writing and 20% content. A good alliance.

Did you make any mistakes when you were setting up? Were there any howlers??

Howlers – not really. Mistakes – not enough investment in my support team early on and not enough focus on building strategic alliances.

What's your key to success?

Activity – I get off my butt and go out.

What advice would you give to new coaches who want a wide range of clients and don't want to be 'pigeon-holed' as a certain type of coach/the coach for a certain type of client?

Don't be stupid – get pigeon holed in a community that has:

- Something that's painful enough to worry them – getting clients, staying alive in a changing market;
- There is a list of them that you can access (there's a list of dentists, there's no list of people who are stressed);
- There is a solution that you know how to deliver;
- They have the money to pay for the solution.

What is your ideal client like?

Apart from the above – we have three golden rules – we trust them, we respect them and we like them. No matter how much money is needed or is on the table, every time I break that rule I make misery for myself. No messers, no prima donnas, no moaners.

Any final thoughts?

It takes 3-5 years to build a viable practice – don't give up your day job.

COACH FILE

Name: Joanne Mallon

Niche: The Media Coach

Website: www.medialifecoach.com

How did you choose your niche?

I feel that my niche chose me. I had been coaching for a few years with no particular niche when I took a break for maternity leave. During that time I did a lot of analyzing of my business: what was and wasn't working, where did I want to go next etc. I realized that the clients I worked best with, and the people who particularly liked working with me, were media professionals, particularly female freelance journalists. I had also always had lots of people in coaching and other businesses coming to me for coaching in media skills. All roads seem to lead to media for me! So I bought the domain name medialifecoach.com and updated my website to reflect this. I had done a talk to my local coaching group about working with the media when I was 8 months pregnant, so when I came back off maternity leave one of the first things I did was develop this into a one day workshop.

Did you have a niche right from the start?

When I got started in coaching people didn't talk about niching – marketing was much more general and we were encouraged to think in terms of our ideal client. So I started off thinking of coaching parents of young children but that didn't particularly take-off. People are familiar with parent coaching now but five years ago it was just too new. I found that it was easy to get coverage in the parenting press, but not so easy to secure the clients. But whilst I was doing this publicity, I found that the journalists that interviewed me were often the ones who became the clients.

When did you realize that having a niche would help you to market yourself?

It took about two years. At first I was quite reluctant to narrow myself down to one particular group, but I think that when you reach the right niche for you it does somehow feel right.

Also it made the marketing more straightforward as all I had to do was concentrate on getting known amongst female media professionals, rather than everybody in the world who might possibly be interested in coaching.

How long did it take for you to establish yourself as 'the' coach for that niche?

Not that long as I was already very associated with media, and there are not too many coaches working in this field. As far as I know I am the only coach in the world who particularly specializes in coaching women in media. In coaching circles I think I am the best known media coach simply because I've been around longest!

What have you learned most about marketing yourself as a coach?

That it is a process, not an event – marketing is something which every business has to do consistently. Therefore it makes sense to stick with the marketing activities that you enjoy enough to keep doing regularly for the life of your business.

How much of a difference did it make when you could promote yourself as a published writer/speaker as well as a coach?

I sometimes speak about writing to promote the business, so I guess it gives it authenticity that my writing is regularly published in newspapers, magazines and websites. I find that potential clients like it if they have heard about me beforehand, whether that's through publications or any other media outlet.

Did you make any mistakes when you were setting up? Were there any howlers??

No real howlers, it's all been good learning. I did get some leaflets printed and spent a couple of days taking them round gyms in the posh parts of London. That yielded precisely one client – a year later. I still have about 100 of those leaflets in a box in my wardrobe. Another early cock-up was when there was a glowing article about me in *The Guardian*. I cleared my diary and waited for the flurry of phone calls.

Unfortunately there were none because the paper had managed to print someone else's contact details under the piece!! Over time that article has been very useful to me because it's such a positive testimonial, but at the time I was very disappointed. This year's cock-ups have involved free session vouchers which I donated to be given to people in my target group attending two separate events. At the first event, the organizer forgot to give them out, and they ended up in the dustbin. At the second event they were given out but hardly anybody redeemed them.

One of the attendees later told me she was saving her voucher for when she really needed it, so my mistake in that instance was not putting an expiry date.

What's your key to success?

Having a clear niche and keeping my profile high so that when potential clients are ready to work with me they will be able to find me easily. Having regular newsletters: www.joannemallon.com/newsletters.htm and starting a networking group for my target clients: www.MediaWomenUK.com.

What advice would you give to new coaches who want a wide range of clients and don't want to be 'pigeon-holed' as a certain type of coach/the coach for a certain type of client?

Even if you don't want a niche, as you are a unique individual, you may very well find that a niche wants you. Put yourself in your potential client's shoes and ask if you would rather employ a generalist or a specialist. I would pick no more than two or three areas that you are interested in coaching people on. Give yourself permission not to choose a niche at first – just play with it and you will soon get a sense of what is calling you.

What is your ideal client like?

Female media professional, aged 25-35, probably working in or near London, ready to move to the next level in her career but not sure how to do so. Or for business media coaching: a person running a small business who wants to raise their media profile and attract publicity.

Any final thoughts?

Check that your proposed niche actually has a track-record in paying for services similar to yours. One challenge that I have found is that whilst I enjoy working with freelance writers, many of them are somewhat financially challenged, and so can find it a struggle to pay coaching fees.

COACH FILE

Name: Nicola Cairncross

Niche: Wealth Coaching

Website: www.themoneygym.com

How did you choose your niche?

They say your niche chooses you and to a degree this is exactly what happened to me. I read about coaching in a newspaper career section and I found a life coach – Rachel Turner – to help with my music management career and it was only when I was made redundant (the music biz is notorious for it's insecurity!) that I considered training as a coach myself. It fit all my criteria – artist management is very similar to coaching except you do a lot of the work! It enabled me to stop commuting and spend more time with my little kids. I originally trained with Coach U and thought I would coach entrepreneurs (as I am one). However, we were deeply in debt and never ever had enough money, although I was bright, energetic and very capable, I just couldn't understand why we were always skint. I looked around and realized that other people must be thinking about and relating to money very differently to me, and getting very different results. Even my coaching business was following the same old pattern – ten clients one month, none the next. I became more and more fascinated in the whole abundance/wealth creation topic. Reading 'Rich Dad Poor Dad', as my coach Rachel had been recommending for months, changed my life completely. Then, as is always the way, the universe sent some amazing people my way and I started learning some life-changing stuff about money, wealth creation, abundance, our attitudes to all of that... and I naturally started to pass it on to my life coaching clients.

Did you have a niche right from the start?

Not really, unless you count wanting to coach small business owners/ entrepreneurs. Then I heard more about niching in the Coach U classes and set myself up as The Music Coach.

I aimed at the business people in the music industry, because I realized that they could afford coaching more than the struggling artists – and I had some success with that, but no referrals as it's a very macho industry and nobody wanted anyone to know their success was not self-generated.

When did you realize that having a niche would help you to market yourself?

My new wealth coaching niche was developing despite me, due to my personal interests and quest to sort my own money issues out, when I realized that I could do with some coaching on not being afraid to ask for the business at the end of the coaching conversation. My coach Rachel Turner recommended Chris Barrow as the best sales coach in the business, and that's how I ended up in rooms full of dentists for three years! He didn't coach coaches in those days but he had a brilliant coaching system that worked and he gave me permission to plagiarize his system.

How long did it take for you to establish yourself as 'the' coach for that niche?

Not long at all! Maybe because I'm very active online and I'm not afraid of poking my head above the parapet, as I call it, on the coach lists. I always say that I'm sensitive with a thick skin. While I like my close friends to think well of me, I'm not scared of people I don't know thinking badly of me, so I just take risks, get on with things that might scare some people. Speaking, writing articles, contributing to forums, appearing on the radio and TV... well, I just feel the fear and do it anyway.

What have you learned most about marketing yourself as a coach?

Loads! And it stands true for all businesses, not just coaches. The most important thing I want to share is that if someone has a problem or some pain, and you have a solution for that problem or pain, then it's up to you to do EVERYTHING you can to communicate this to that person. You are actually doing them a big disservice if you remain a secret to your potential clients. You need to get on a total mission to find those people, tell them clearly and simply that you can help them and then not be ashamed to exchange your energy and coaching skills for their energy (cash).

This is all marketing is, really. Don't put obstacles in their way when they want to buy – it's incredible how many of us do that subconsciously. To make it easy for your potential clients, I've learned that you have to package up coaching into various price points (programmes), because open-ended coaching scares people. They somehow feel that they might get 'dependent' on their coach and that scares them. You need to give people a real feel for who you are via your website/blog/ezine – but direct all your marketing on your site at the reader and don't bang on about you all the time. They are NOT INTERESTED in you, your college, your qualifications or memberships - only whether you understand their situation and their pain/problem and if you can help them. They also want proof. Also, don't try to do marketing things you don't really enjoy or which don't bring the results you want. I love meeting new people so networking was fun for me, but I rarely attracted clients by this method. But I did build my 'Dream Team' of bank manager, accountant, solicitor and insurance broker that way. However, it's very time consuming and you are only getting in front of a few people at a time. The internet is great for coaches because you can get in front of the 35 million people on broadband right now! Google ensures that if you have a great niche, you can attract visitors to your new site within 15 minutes and then test whether your marketing system is working very quickly. I decided very early on that my main marketing focus would be online because I had always been fascinated by the web and, in fact, I had a little music biz website already. With Chris' guidance, I created three versions of the same programme with three price levels with the lower two being automated. I created a one year programme to avoid the 'churn' factor. I put my prices on the site for each level so I didn't have to have THAT conversation and folks knew before they came what their investment would be.

How much of a difference did it make when you could promote yourself as an author/speaker as well as a coach?

The speaking definitely helps as it attracts a few very interested potential future clients to your mailing list. Many of my clients said later, "Oh I saw you speak at ______ and joined your mailing list". But you have to have a way to keep these new people warm and an ezine is crucial for that. I haven't sold enough copies of my book yet to make a huge difference but the fact that its on my site and in my email signature, and it's on Amazon and in Waterstones etc. certainly gives me credibility. People have a respect for someone who has managed to write a book and get it published – it's getting easier and easier nowadays. I wrote mine in tiny chunks, day by day. It was an e-programme first. I planned it out first, then got an R&D team to experience it day-by-day, give me feedback, pick up typos and bits that were not so clear. A Thomas Leonard idea – what a genius that man was.

Did you make any mistakes when you were setting up? Were there any howlers??

Were there!? Where do I start?! Taking on my first client without realizing that she was seeing me on her days out from the long-term mental hospital where she had been having treatment for depression. I was hired by the husband and although he said I made a huge difference I've always felt that I shouldn't have taken her on. Not asking people at the end of introductory calls if/when they wanted to start. Not being there for coaching calls was my worst fault. I always had so much going on I used to totally forget about the calls! Funnily enough two of the clients who had the worst experience with that went on to do incredibly well with the Money Gym and then became my business partners. I now say that I was testing their perseverance – a required quality for wealth creation! Then I started using the online diary system **www.GetCaughtOnTime.com** and that corralled my clients into certain times on certain days. So I sat at my desk between those times on those days. If I wasn't coaching, I was marketing. It also allowed clients to make, cancel and change their own appointments, thus eliminating a lot of the admin/email to'ing and fro'ing.

What advice would you give to new coaches who want a wide range of clients and don't want to be 'pigeon-holed' as a certain type of coach/the coach for a certain type of client?

Listen, you don't have to get your niche tattooed on your forehead! You will eventually attract a wide range of clients because your 'niche' clients will recommend you to their friends and colleagues. But aiming at a niche initially makes it so much easier to target your marketing. I aimed at people who wanted to know how money works, but many of the people I end up working with now are very wealthy. They are always looking to learn, you see. In the early days, do you have the luxury of not wanting to be pigeon holed? Thomas Leonard, in one of his famous 'Personal Foundation' tapes said once that, "you can't afford the luxury of freedom until you can pay the bills." So true.

What is your ideal client like?

First and foremost they must be an action taker. I can't be doing with endless conversations with why someone hasn't done something, I would rather they said, "No, I can't or won't do that" or that they did something, anything and got it wrong, so that we could cross it off the list and move on. I love working with strong women and emotionally intelligent men. Rough diamonds are fab too! I love straight talking people with no 'side' to them – I don't play games. My ideal client has off days, and I hope that I'm kind and supportive while they do, but they usually always want to take action at the end of their laments. They must be open-minded to new ideas as we light so many light bulbs for people, in such a short space of time, that it reminds me of an old fifties sci-fi movie when the actors heads spin round and then explode! Ideally, their partners should be ready for the ride too, as the thing that holds most people back in my experience is having to 'get permission' to take action from their spouse who isn't interested, or worse, negative or hostile.

Final thought

My life is totally unrecognizable now and that's ALL down to coaching. Wow! In just seven years! The most amazing things happen on a daily basis now. The best thing is, I am very ordinary and haven't done anything extraordinary. You can do it too.

COACH FILE

Name: Judith Morgan

Niche: Entrepreneurs & Small Business Owners

Website: www.judithmorgan.com

How did you choose your niche?

Do you know, I am not sure I did choose my niche, I think in the end my niche chose me and I'm very happy with that. To some extent I even resisted my niche because previously I was a small business accountant and, having sold my practice, I thought I wanted a completely fresh start. But I have 30 years' experience of working with small business clients and I know them through and through, and I love them and so it was inevitable I would come home to work with them again. Now that I have started to target myself exclusively at my ideal client, I was going to say my business has really taken off, but that's not what I mean. My business had already really taken off simply with the momentum of throwing everything I had at it for three years, determined to coach. What has caused it to become effortlessly successful is getting really clear on who I want to work with, and making a selection of options and price breaks available to potential clients so that they can choose the most appropriate one for them.

Did you have a niche right from the start?

Nope. In fact, I am to some extent anti-niche, especially for new coaches. I think your first 6-12 months should be spent coaching everyone and anyone that moves, so you get a great deal of experience and coaching hours under your belt, enabling you to become a really confident and competent coach in all ways. Doing this will also help you to move closer to your niche. It also helps you notice who is drawn to work with you and enables you to ask the market what they want you to provide, and then you can sell it back to them. That's very important; always ask your market what they want rather than assuming you know what's good for them based on what you believe they should have and then trying to force it on them.

When did you realize that having a niche would help you to market yourself?

I always believed it would help me market myself. What it does, in effect, is enable you to send out a very clear marketing message which makes it much, much easier for your clients to buy from you.

How long did it take for you to establish yourself as 'the' coach for that niche?

Two to three years. With hindsight, I realize I was moving inexorably towards the day when my niche seemed obvious.

What have you learned most about marketing yourself as a coach?

You have to kiss a lot of frogs! I think you have to throw yourself into everything and try it all and find out what works best for you; PR, workshops, breakfast networking, blogging, articles, newsletters, free introductory sessions, public speaking, advertising, joint ventures, I could go on and on.

Ultimately you have to get clear and create a plan to focus on just three that you feel naturally inclined towards and which, as a result, start to work really well for you. In my own case that was internet marketing, writing and meeting people. I have learned that you have to learn to love marketing. You have to find out what it is and how to make it work for your business, and to create a marketing machine for your business which just rolls on and on to a regular schedule. This helps to smooth out the feast and famine cycle of most businesses where you stop marketing when you have a full practice. Get a waiting list!

Did you make any mistakes when you were setting up? Were there any howlers??

I am sure there were hundreds. Fortunately I am an optimist and a naturally positive thinker and cannot call any to mind! Probably spending too much money on the half of all marketing which they say doesn't work. But I don't regret that. *Je ne regrette rien!*

Of course, I made lots of very useful mistakes when coaching people from which I could learn to be a better coach, I still do. The trick is noticing them immediately and changing tack without missing a beat, so either only you know, or that it becomes somehow useful for your client also.

What's your key to success?

Be prepared to do whatever it takes to be successful in your chosen business. It helps very much if you love what you do and do what you love. Do all that you can with whatever you have from where you are. Work with a great coach. The most important thing for those of us in the entrepreneurial sector is focus. One thing at a time until it is launched and up and running and making profits, before you turn to your next project. Systemize and e-myth your business. Create a Business to Love which stands alone without you, otherwise you are just self-employed which is like having a J.O.B. without the holiday pay, sick pay or pensions! A Business to Love is something you can sell when the time is right. This is trickier in coaching, but far from impossible and you can still coach within that business, if that's what you love. I do.

What advice would you give to new coaches who want a wide range of clients and don't want to be 'pigeon-holed' as a certain type of coach/the coach for a certain type of client?

Couldn't agree more at the outset, as I have said. Ultimately you will get clearer about your ideal client. Deliberately take notice of who you like working with and why. Also who is attracted to work with you and why. A niche will emerge. Doesn't mean you will only attract those clients and the choice is always yours about whether or not to work with them. For instance, you can target your coaching at women and still attract maybe 20% of men. Will you work with them? I would if they were a good fit.

What is your ideal client like?

Self-employed, solopreneur, small business person and/or entrepreneur, working for themselves, possibly at home, trying to do it all themselves, dissipating focus, getting nowhere fast. My ideal client is very motivated to learn how to create a successful and profitable business which also allows them to have a life. Generally they are what I call 'perfectionist control-freaks' who need to learn to ease up, do less, be more and get better results. Clients who want to e-myth their businesses, preferably from the get-go. Clients who are motivated, energetic, with HUGE ambitions to create a Business to Love.

Any final thoughts?

Nobody needs a coach, unlike an accountant, which I was in my previous career. Unless you find a way to distinguish yourself and address your clients' pain, you will wither and die on the vine. Get stuck in and really enjoy your marketing, throw yourself into it whole-heartedly and become a bigger person for it. If you love to coach, learn to love to market yourself. Whatever it takes.

Suggested Reading

Suggested Reading

Here are just some of the books which I have enjoyed over the past couple of years which I think you might get some benefit from reading.

Marketing and influencing skills

"...and death came third: The Definitive Guide to Networking and Speaking in Public", Andy Lopata and Peter Roper, www.BookShaker.com, 2006

"How to Become a Rainmaker: The Rules for Getting and Keeping Customers and Clients", Jeffery J. Fox, Vermilion, 2001

"How to Win Friends and Influence People", Dale Carnegie, Vermilion, 2006

"Marketing the Professional Services Firm: Applying the Principles and the Science of Marketing to the Professions", Laurie Young, John Wiley and Sons Ltd, 2005

"Proper Coffee and Other Ways to Grow Your Business", Hugh Williams, Lawpack Publishing, 2005

Business

"Losing My Virginity: The Autobiography", Richard Branson, Virgin Books, 2005

"Rich Dad, Poor Dad: What the Rich Teach Their Kids About Money That the Poor and the Middle Class Do Not", Robert T. Kiyosaki, Time Warner Paperbacks, 2002

"Sack Your Boss: Quit Your Job and Turn Your Passion into Your Profession", Joanthan Jay, Crown House Publishing, 2005

"Screw It, Let's Do It: Lessons in Life (Quick Reads)" Richard Branson, Virgin Books, 2006

"The E-Myth Revisited", Michael Gerber, HarperCollins, 1994

"The Millionaire Upgrade: Lessons in Success from Those Who Travel at the Sharp End of the Plane", Richard Parkes Cordock, Capstone Publishing Ltd, 2006

"The Tipping Point: How Little Things Can Make a Big Difference", Malcolm Gladwell, Abacus, 2002

Management

"The One Minute Manager", Kenneth Blanchard and Spencer Johnson, HarperCollins Business, 2000

"Who Moved My Cheese?: An Amazing Way to Deal with Change in Your Work and in Your Life", Spencer Johnson, Vermilion, 1999

Coaching and NLP techniques

"Coaching for Performance", Sir John Whitmore, Nicholas Brealey Publishing Ltd, 2002

"Effective Coaching: Lessons from the coach's coach", Myles Downey, Textere Publishing, 2003

"Neuro-Linguistic Programming for Dummies", Romilla Ready, John Wiley and Sons Ltd, 2004

"The Life Coaching Handbook: Everything You Need to Be an Effective Life Coach", Curly Martin, Crown House Publishing, 2001